The Great Acting Teachers and Their Methods

A Smith and Kraus Book
Published by Smith and Kraus, Inc.
Hanover, NH 03755
smithandkraus.com

Manufactured in the United States of America

Cover and Text Design by Julia Hill Gignoux
illustrations by Deborah Stevenson

First Edition: December 1995
1

Library of Congress Cataloging-in-Publication Data

Brestoff, Richard.
The great acting teachers and their methods / by Richard Brestoff.
1st ed. p. cm. -- (Career development series)
Includes bibliographical references and index.
ISBN-10 1-57525-012-8 ISBN-13: 978-1-57525-012-0
1. Acting--Study and teaching. I. Title. II. Series.
PN2075.B674 1995
792'.028'07--dc20 95-26289
CIP

THE GREAT ACTING TEACHERS and Their Methods

by Richard Brestoff

illustrations by Deborah Stevenson

A Career Development Book

SK

A Smith and Kraus Book

RICHARD BRESTOFF

Actor and teacher Richard Brestoff has acted on Broadway and Off, in Regional theater, and in film, television and radio. He is a Phi Beta Kappa graduate of the University of California's Dramatic Art Department at Berkeley, and holds an M.F.A. in acting from New York University's School of the Arts. He is a student of Master Teacher Peter Kass, to whom his first book *The Camera Smart Actor* is dedicated. His many other teachers include, Olympia Dukakis, Joseph Chaikin, Kristin Linklater, Omar Shapli, Nora Dunfee and Gary Schwartz. He currently teaches in the Seattle area, and can be reached at his e-mail address: RBrestoff@aol.com.

Dedication

I wish to dedicate this book to Deborah Stevenson for her talent, her help and her understanding, to Jenny Stevenson-Brestoff for her forbearance, and to the spirits of two who will be dearly missed: Ms. Nora Dunfee, and Ms. Viola Spolin.

I would like to thank Eric Kraus and Marisa Smith for suggesting this book to me, teacher and actress Robyn Hunt for her generosity and insight, librarian Liz Fugate of the University of Washington for her expert guidance, actress and teacher Johanna Melamed for her thoughtful help, actress Susan Williams for her valuable comments, and of course my teachers Peter Kass, Olympia Dukakis, Joe Chaikin, Kristin Linklater, Nora Dunfee, Omar Shapli, and Gary Schwartz.

❊

This book is one actor/teacher's personal and imaginative response to some of the greatest thinkers and theatrical practitioners that the world of acting has yet known.

Table of Contents

Dedication v

Introduction ix

❄

Chapter 1 *Acting May Be Hazardous To Your Health!* 1

Chapter 2 *The Russian Revolution* 16

Chapter 3 *Smashing The Fourth Wall* 59

Chapter 4 *The American Revolution* 77

Chapter 5 *Lee Strasberg* 93

Chapter 6 *Stella Adler* 117

Chapter 7 *Sanford Meisner* 128

Chapter 8 *Viola Spolin and the Theater of Games* 139

Chapter 9 *Bertold Brecht and the Theater of Politics* 147

Chapter 10 *Jerzy Grotowski and the Holy Actor* 154

Chapter 11 *Tadashi Suzuki and the Theater of Grandeur* 163

Chapter 12 *Training School Profiles* 169

Actor's Studio/New School *171*

American Conservatory Theater *172*

American Repertory Theater *173*

California Institute of the Arts *174*

Columbia University *175*

Herbert Berghof Studios *176*

Juilliard School *177*

New Actor's Workshop *179*

New York University *180*

Northwestern University *181*

Stella Adler Conservatory-New York *183*

University of Illinois-Urbana *184*

University of Washington *185*

University of Wisconsin-Milwaukee *186*

Yale University *187*

❄

Conclusions 188

Endnotes 191

Bibliography 197

Video Bibliography 202

Index 203

Introduction

2,500 years ago the first actor of the Western world stepped out from the Greek Chorus and into history. When Thespis of Icaria separated himself from his troupe and enacted the role of the tragic hero, he occasioned a revolution. No longer were events being recounted from a distant perspective, from the third person point of view, now, the actual character was represented in the *first* person, acting and talking before the audience through the body of an actor. This created a sensation in the provinces of Greece where Thespis first appeared. But when he and his troupe came to the great city of Athens, the reception was somewhat cooler.

Solon, a Greek wise man and legislator, had heard about Thespis's innovations and decided to see for himself what this new phenomenon was all about. So, one day in Athens in 534 b.c., he went to witness one of Thespis's performances. What he saw disturbed him so much, that he confronted Thespis afterwards. He demanded to know why Thespis was not ashamed to tell so many lies before so many people. Thespis replied that such lying was harmless so long as it was done in play. Solon angrily struck his staff to the ground and exclaimed, "yes, but if we allow ourselves to praise and honor make-believe like this, the next thing will be to find it creeping into our serious business." [1]

Acting's first critic objected to the act of acting itself. Indeed, Solon's words haunt us when we acknowledge how often politicians, Chief Executive Officers, lawyers and others avail themselves of the expertise of acting coaches in order to help them appear more palatable and convincing to their audiences. Lying in public seems to have become a national past time. And yet is this really the fault of Thespis?

The art of acting has not taught the world to lie. People have done so since the beginning of time. And if acting in a play *is* lying, then we simply do not see that lie as destructive. Rather, we regard that lie as Picasso defined all of art, as "the lie that reveals a deeper truth."

Transformation has something of the magical about it. And the great power of an actor to become someone else holds a mesmeric fascination over those who do it and those who watch it. Actors and directors have written about it, psychologists, philosophers, social scientists, and even biologists have pondered it. What is acting, and how is it done? How does someone become someone else? *Can* someone become someone else? How much of what an actor does is due to that mysterious quality we call *talent?* Does an actor lose himself into a character, or are the actor and the role separate? How does the actor free his emotions? Should an actor use his emotions? How is acting different from real life? How important is believability? Does an actor act from the "outside in," or from the "inside out"? How can the actor stay spontaneous when he must repeat a performance night after night? Is acting an art or a craft? What type of training does an actor need? *Can* acting be taught?

These questions have occupied the great teachers and theorists of acting for over 2500 years, giving rise to passionate, at times, vicious arguments between partisans of one view or another. Dominant theories and strong countercurrents have contended with one another throughout the history of acting.

For centuries the great argument in acting has centered on Presentational versus Representational styles. Or, in other words, should the actor *present* the character or try to *become* the character? This opposition is sometimes seen as the difference between the use of physical techniques to portray a character or inner psychological ones (this difference has been characterized as the British versus the American approach). These distinctions are debated endlessly. Were Shakespeare's actors realistic or presentational? The truth is, no one really knows. None of us was there.

Most of us judge actors from the past by performances we have seen in early silent films. And when we watch some of the excessive eye-bugging and mustache twirling, we paint the entire past history of acting with that broad brush. We assume that acting before our time was overly theatrical, bombastically false, and hugely funny. We condemn earlier styles of performance as totally alien to our modern ways. We feel that earlier ideas about acting and our own are simply incompatible.

And yet a dispassionate survey of the great ideas about acting shows a remarkable and surprising agreement. All the major western theories about acting propose that actors integrate the use of their bodies, minds, voices, imaginations and emotions to expressive ends. There has always been a link between the actor's inner life and its outer expression.

It is a mistake of oversimplification to believe that the actors of the 18th century cared nothing about being "real," or that today's teachers of the Method care nothing about the voice. In the 18th century, the great English actor David Garrick had a wig specially constructed so that when his Hamlet saw the ghost of his father, his hair would appear to stand on end. Why? In the hopes of creating a more realistic appearance of fright and shock. Few actors would think to go this far. Lee Strasberg, the main teacher of Method acting, advocated forcefully that actors acquire a powerful and flexible vocal technique capable of carrying the expressive content of passionate emotion. The usual notions about acting styles are clearly too simplistic. And yet differences among them *do* exist.

These differences arise as to *how* to train and use the body, *how* to train and use the voice and mind, and *how* to open up and use the actor's emotional life.

But times and tastes and conditions change. What was good acting to some, becomes bad acting to others. One generation's truth, becomes another generation's cliché. And so, new ideas and theories are born. Sometimes change comes from an actor who has seen a better way, sometimes it comes from a playwright whose work demands a new style. Sometimes change comes from a designer whose sets inspire a new approach to performance. Change may come from a director whose unique vision requires a new style of acting. However it comes, change is inevitable. Actors we consider perfect today, will almost certainly be seen as flawed tomorrow. If this were not so, the art of acting would petrify. But this dynamic vitality, this constant evolution, which keeps the art of acting a living thing, exacts a price.

All the years of passionate struggle to understand the elusive essence of acting, has resulted in a bewildering array of systems, methods, theories and techniques. The actor is left with many questions: University training, or private study? Lee Strasberg, or Stella Adler? How is one to choose? Who, are these people? What do they teach, and how did their ideas evolve?

Most of the important teachers of acting have been actors themselves. They have grappled with the real world demands of their art and tried to extend its boundaries. They have intensely examined the process of acting and dedicated their lives to penetrating its mysteries. They have built upon the foundations laid down by their predecessors.

Most private acting teachers today are either students of these great master teachers, or were students of their students. And most teachers teach as they were taught. A student of Stella Adler's will teach her work, with minor variations. You teach what you know. But it must be admitted that some of the magic of these great teachers is, or was, in them alone. Is the Actor's Studio as good a training institution without Lee Strasberg, or was its power due to the presence of Strasberg himself? Strasberg very much wanted to believe that the brilliance and effectiveness of his methods would survive him. But that remains to be seen.

In the college and university training programs, the emphasis is different. In many universities there is an open hostility to so-called Method acting, although they will often have teachers trained in the various versions of the Stanislavsky system. Colleges and universities incorporate methods taken from many sources. Masks will be used, and voice, movement and speech will be taught. In some places, the work of Tadashi Suzuki is being offered. Each training institution has its own unique offerings and emphases.

With so many options, what should an actor do? Should he gather a representative sampling of many approaches, collecting various tools for his acting toolbox? Or should he study one method in depth in the hopes of acquiring a single and coherent acting method? Most acting teachers would say that acquiring a complete technique requires both approaches. A single training system has the advantage of giving the actor a way to approach his craft step-by-step. But since no single system can possibly contain all that might be helpful to an actor, the student must also gather what tools he can from other sources.

But even after an actor has chosen his path of study, he still faces more questions. Is this the best teacher for him? Are these exercises truly effective? Is he growing as an actor? The actor must continually evaluate his progress. And this evaluation is made more difficult by the fact that most training is *a*historical. That is, the student is rarely told how the exercises he is doing evolved, or from what traditions they come. Individual acting classes are given without much reference to the context of actor training as a whole.

It is vital for actors to understand how their craft evolved and in what tradition they stand. A global understanding of the past and present orients one better towards the future. It is important to know that realism in acting came as a reaction to the falseness that had gone before. Knowing this, one can anticipate that realism too will be overthrown in its turn. For example, in many private studios and at universities today, body training and mask work is in the ascendancy.

Making one's way through the maze of actor training is a daunting task. This book is designed to help you understand the most important ideas about acting, where they came from, and how they are used in training programs today. With this knowledge, you will be prepared to make wise choices about your own path through this rewarding, frustrating, astonishing art.

"The theater is a sea of human forces." NERO

Chapter 1

Acting May Be Hazardous To Your Health!

An actor, rehearsing the role of a madman, loses his mind. Another, playing a character with gout, contracts the disease. Yet another, following a performance, continues to believe himself an Emperor. True stories? Certainly not.

Yet stories like these have circulated for thousands of years, painting actors as vulnerable to a strange kind of possession. It is as though, having put on the mask of transformation, the actor cannot remove it. The attributes and maladies of the "character" migrate across some imperceptible barrier, seep into the fiber of his being and endanger both the actor's health and sanity.

Believe it or not, this view, of a dangerous interaction between character and actor, has had a powerful impact on the practice of acting. Like the shaman, who takes on the illness of those he cures, the actor has been considered slightly crazy for deliberately putting himself in harm's way. But how, we wonder, does acting put anyone in danger? What is the source of this harm?

For over 1,800 years, it was believed that powerful feelings could cause illness and that illness, in turn, could cause powerful passions. Emotions themselves were not considered to be natural, organic, or even healthy. This idea, of course, puts the actor in a difficult position since his job is to enact strong feeling. What, we wonder, is the source of this crippling belief that emotions can make us sick?

The human body was thought by the Greeks to be composed of four basic fluids just as the Universe itself was composed of four basic elements. Emotion, it was believed, was caused by a stirring up and rebalancing of these fluids, just as motion itself was caused by the mixing of the four basic elements. The word "emotion" means, in Latin, to stir up; to agitate. It was believed that when these fluids were jolted into an imbalance, an illness occurred accompanied by a strong passion, known as a Humour.

Emotion, then, was often seen as a symptom of an internal problem. Now before we judge this explanation of human feeling as foolish, it would be wise to remember that today we believe chemical imbalances to be responsible for clinical depression and emotional stress. And we believe that this inner stress can indeed make us sick. The idea that the body influences the mind and that the mind influences the body, is one that the science of our own day confirms.

But now, let us take a closer look at this particular, ancient view of the mind-body connection.

The four vital fluids in the human body were said to be these: black bile, yellow bile, red blood and phlegm. They were related to the four basic elements of the Universe: Earth, Fire, Air and Water. In this way, the body mirrored the Universe.

If too much *black bile* was present in one's body, gloom, sadness and feelings of morbidity resulted. One man with too much black bile was said to have swum across a canal in order to throw himself under a train. Such a person was said to be in a *Melancholic* humour. Today, we might refer to one of our friends as being in a "black" mood.

If too much *yellow bile* was present, anger resulted. A person given to great rages was said to be of a *Choleric* disposition.

An overabundance of *red blood* caused one to become amorous, cheerful, courageous, hopeful and confident. Red cheeks were characteristic of one in this condition which was known as a *Sanguine* humour. Today, we might refer to such a person as feeling "in the pink."

Having too much *phlegm* (mucous) made a person sluggish and apathetic, and such a person was said to be *Phlegmatic*. The following chart shows these relationships:

Element	**Fluid**	**Emotion**	**Humour**
Earth	Black Bile	Sadness	Melancholy
Fire	Yellow Bile	Anger	Choleric
Air	Red Blood	Cheerfulness	Sanguine
Water	Phlegm	Apathy	Phlegmatic

Imagine the dilemma this system poses for an actor. If he uses his own deep feelings to express the emotions of a character, he runs the risk of triggering an imbalance in his body, which could then cause a life threatening illness.

What is an actor to do? Not feel real feelings? That couldn't be right. In fact, one of the cardinal rules of effective performance laid down in Roman times was this: "the prime essential for stirring the emotions of others is...first to feel those emotions oneself."[1] So an actor is to feel real feelings, but not so much so as to endanger himself. How could this be done?

What was needed was a safe way for actors to portray intense emotion without literally being "carried away." Safeguards were required. And they were provided.

It was believed that each emotion had a specific physical manifestation. Gestures, facial expressions, vocal inflections, body poses and body movements together or separately could communicate any inner feeling. What was needed was a set of rules that told the actor which physical expressions corresponded to which emotional ones. In this way, the actor could represent the inner feeling by doing something physical.

A system of body and sign language was developed that could be clearly "read" and understood by the audience. This protected the actor from the danger of having to directly experience strong passions, and yet still enable him to communicate what was going on inside the character. The first comprehensive attempt to provide this necessary language was made in the first century A.D. by a Roman teacher of Rhetoric named Quintilian.

Now, in Roman times and throughout the Middle Ages, Rhetoric meant more than just speech making. It encompassed the entire education of an informed adult. Orators were even used to argue cases before judges although they were not specifically trained in the law. Lawyers handled the actual legal matters, but often called upon orators to make final pleas before judges, hoping that their impassioned eloquence would sway a verdict. Quintilian was heavily involved in such work. So it must be kept in mind that his system for portraying emotion is meant to persuade a judge; that is, it is entirely *audience* directed. His rules were followed and quoted by actors well into the Renaissance, and still have some currency today. So what secrets of expression did Quintilian pass on to public performers? What language did he create?

Natural expressions of feeling, writes Quintilian, are good because they are sincere, but they are not really useful because they are devoid of art. Feelings which are imitated or artificial are less sincere, but more artful and are therefore to be preferred.

Now, says Quintilian, if one imagines a real feeling, then the voice will naturally express the required emotion. If one imagines anger, the voice will be "fierce, rough and thick." If one imagines pity, the voice will be "tender and mournful." These notions don't seem too foreign to us today. We know that when we speak from feeling, it colors our voices. A strong, clear, articulate voice is as important to us today as it was to Quintilian 2000 years ago.

What about the body? To study gesture (which for him is a kind of emotional sign language), Quintilian suggests the use of a large mirror. A mirror which will appear again and again in the study of acting and come to haunt the actor of the 20th century.

Without a mirror, people cannot see their own faces. Our eyes are placed in such a way that doing so is impossible. How lucky we are! Imagine if we could monitor our every reaction, watch ourselves eat, and see ourselves talk? Wouldn't we become excruciatingly self-conscious? Before mirrors, the only way we could see ourselves was by gazing into a clear pool, and isn't that what got Narcissus into so much trouble? Are we meant to be so hyper-aware of what our faces are doing as we live our everyday lives? Probably not. But, let's follow Quintilian's advice, and push on.

Now, in this mirror, one practices gestures and studies their accuracy. But the question is, which gestures should one practice? Let's start with the head.

Go stand in front of a mirror. Quintilian says that casting down the head shows humility. Try it. Did you look humble? Now keep your head "rigid and unmoved." According to Quintilian you should now be expressing rudeness. Do you look rude? Are you starting to feel silly? Just a Rhetorical question. Another rule is that "the face must always be turned in the same direction as the gesture, except in speaking of things of which we disapprove." Seem arbitrary? Anyway, back to the mirror.

Raise your hand slightly, and with each of the fingers curved, slowly open and close your hand. This, says Quintilian is useful for expressing admiration. Also, you must not raise your hand above the eyes or let it fall below the chest and you must never gesture with the left hand alone.

Now, take a look at your whole body. Keep in mind what Quintilian says, "take care that the breast and stomach be not too much protruded; for such an attitude bends the back inwards; and, besides, all bending backwards is offensive." What do you think? Do you look offensive? Back to the hand. Draw the middle finger in toward the thumb and keep the other three fingers open. This is a good position, according to Quintilian, for stating facts. Now, curve your hands gently, move them a bit back and forth allowing the shoulders to move with them. This motion shows us a person who is reserved and timid. There is some truth in this one isn't there? Try it.

Before we make all of this sound too ridiculous, it must be noted that Quintilian also said this: "the movement of the hand should begin and end with the sense...Gesture should be suited rather to sense than to words." But even while believing this, he gives us rules that have more to do with custom than sense. And though most of these rules are meant for orators, actors have taken them as gospel truth for generations. There are rules for the neck, eyes, eyebrows, nose, forehead, lips; "to lick and bite them is unbecoming," arms, throat, chin, feet, and shoulders; shrugging them is a gesture of meanness. In order to avoid doing it, one orator practiced his speeches with a spear hanging down over one shoulder so that he would be reminded not to raise his shoulders "by a puncture from the weapon." True dedication.

Quintilian succeeded in creating a physical way to express emotions without asking the performer to delve too deeply into his own dangerous personal feelings.

But this multitude of rules is confining. It puts the actor in a straitjacket, and make his gestures and moves too self-conscious. Quintilian was, no doubt, a superb orator and used the techniques he wrote about. And yet, it seems as if there is only one kind of anger, or sadness, or humility, or rudeness to be expressed in this system. What about the anger spoken in low tones or with a clenched smile? What about the rudeness of not looking someone in the eye?

What strikes us as particularly odd about Quintilian's system, is that feelings are expressed in standardized ways. The great variety of human expression is absent. It is strange to think that feelings, the most irrational and subjective parts of our makeup could be reduced to single, definable, modes of expression. And yet, that is what Quintilian's "language" does. And in prescribing this system for others, he helped to create an artificial style of acting that petrified the art for ages.

It must be said, however, that there were talented actors throughout history who were able to fill the prescribed gestures with a sense of believability and inner truth. Such artists have existed in all ages, transcending the limited techniques of their times.

How influential were Quintilian's words? How far was his reach? Let's leap ahead some 1700 years and take a look.

❊

It is now 1753, the middle of the 18th century. We are standing in a book shop in England holding a pamphlet by the actor, director and critic, Aaron Hill. It is called *The Art of Acting: An Essay.* And lo and behold one of the first things he asks the actor to do is to find a mirror! Quintilian's reach is long. 1700 years have passed and actors are still staring into mirrors. We begin reading the essay.

Hill tells us that there are ten, and only ten, dramatic passions. They are: joy, grief, anger, pity, scorn, hatred, jealousy, wonder, fear, and love. That's it. He then goes on to tell us how to enact each one. We notice a mirror at the back of the shop and head over to it. Are you there? Good. Let's do "joy."

First, Hill wants us to imagine the idea of joy and "impress" it onto our facial muscles. Sound like Quintilian? Look into the mirror. O.K., we are now impressing joy onto our face. If the brow appears bent downwards, or the chest is not "thrown gracefully back," then we are doing it incorrectly. If, however, our forehead appears open, and raised, and our eyes are smiling and sparkling, and our neck is stretched and erect without stiffness, our arms, wrists fingers, hip, knees and ankles "braced boldly," we are doing it right. Joy is being expressed. What do you think? Do you look joyful? If so, Hill advises you to imitate yourself exactly whenever you are required to show joy. That imitation will then appear to others as natural.

How about grief? Simple: "The muscles must fall loose and be unbraced. Speak, and the voice will then follow, sounding naturally full of misery and anguish." Here we find Quintilian again. He too said to imagine the feeling first, and then to speak.

Fear? Fear is a mixture. Assume the same slack muscles as used in grief but (are you standing in front of the mirror?) add a startled look to your face. Keep the "eyes widely stretched but unfixed, the mouth still and open." When you speak, a fearful tone will naturally color your voice.

Anger is also a mixture. As in joy, tense the muscles, add a flashing to the eye, set the teeth, expand the nostrils wide, bend the eye brow, "and hold hard the breath." Try it. This is an exhausting one isn't it?

We put the book down for a minute to catch our breath and think. This author seems intent on providing a recipe book of emotional expressions. We know that by this time in history, no one really believes in the four humours anymore. Strong feelings are no longer regarded with the same fear and suspicion as they were previously. And yet actors are still being asked to imitate generic emotions with standardized poses. Why? Part of the answer is a continued belief in the words of Quintilian. But part of the answer lies elsewhere.

The 18th century was the age of the machine. And machines can be made to imitate almost anything. Human beings were regarded quite simply as "wondrous" machines, who could feign real emotions and fool any observer. It became an obsession to reproduce real feelings and effects (blushing, sweating, suddenly turning pale) through imitation. So, the mirror becomes an even more important and necessary weapon in the actor's arsenal than ever.

Imitation even meant the imitation of other actors. Most new actors were trained by watching and then copying the actors whose roles best suited them. If you were to be the young lover, you watched and copied the actor currently playing the young lover. Does this strike a chord? How many actors have you seen imitating James Dean or Jack Nicholson, or Goldie Hawn, today? Maybe you've even done it yourself. But, let that go.

Imitation went even further. Actors began copying the poses found in paintings. They would even brag to each other about how well they copied the position of a character in a certain painting and then how effectively they used it on the stage.

We pick up the acting book again. How, we wonder, should we imitate pity? By the way, did we happen to catch a glimpse of ourselves while we "wondered"? Will it correspond to Aaron Hill's description of how wonder should be expressed? Just wondering. Back to pity.

To imitate pity, you first strain the muscles into tension, add the look which is proper to pity, which is the face of sorrow combined with the "spring on the muscles adopted to joy," and immediately the gestures, voice and feelings will be those of pity. Were you able to combine sorrow and joy on your face?

How about hatred? Perhaps you didn't know this, but there is "no difference but the turn of an eye in the expression of hatred and pity." You use the "same intense brace upon the joints and sinews, but with pity you look at the person with a face impressed with goodness, and with anger you turn away from them with a face reflecting an image of...evil." How about that. Practice alternating between pity and anger. Does it work? Aren't we back to Quintilian, using pre-determined body positions and facial expressions to represent generic emotions? Of course we are. And part of the reason for this is that the characters being played are gods or goddesses, or kings, queens, princes and princesses. These elevated members of society should not act or look like common folk. They must be better. They must be enacted "beautifully."

"Beauty is truth," wrote John Keats and that was the actor's new credo. If acting was beautiful, then it was, by definition, truthful. These gestures, expressions and ways of holding the body were meant to portray "beautiful" anger, "beautiful" pity, "beautiful" grief, "beautiful" jealousy, and so on.

What about wonder? Wonder is shown with muscles intense, awful alarm in the eye, a step backwards, and an intake of breath. We've seen silent movie actors do this very thing when startled.

Love? Love is done with muscles intense, and a respectful attachment in the eye. In scorn, the muscles are slack and there is a smile in the eye. And to show jealousy, the muscles are intense again, the look pensive, or, the look is intense and the muscles slack.

That's it. The ten passions and how to play them. So then, actors of the time are doing their jobs by copying the pre-planned gestures, movements and facial expressions of others, doing it beautifully and, of course, practicing it all in front of a mirror.

Yet we must give Aaron Hill his due. He does have some new and different ideas. For one, he believed in true emotion. For another, he rebelled against Quintilian's audience directed performing style. Hill's advice is that, "...whenever you can forget an audience, you will charm them. In order to warm every body who sees you act, you need only to forget that you are acting."[2] But still, he relies on standardized expressions and gestures to convey emotional meaning.

Did no one fight this system? Did no one want to break free of these expressive restraints? Did no one see through the artificiality of it all? Someone did. But not who you think.

We look at the mirror before us and see a shadowy figure in it. We look closer. The figure is gesturing to us. What is this? The figure invites us into the mirror and we step forward. What's going on?

❄

Instantly we find ourselves in an auditorium, and by the sound of the man speaking on stage, we have, with a single step, crossed from England to France. The shadowy figure is nowhere to be seen.

On the floor we spy a program and bend to pick it up. For some unexplainable reason we are able to read the French words perfectly and understand the French speech we hear. Later, we're going to have to take a closer look at that mirror.

The program tells us that the man on stage is François Delsarte. It tells us that he studied acting at the Royal Dramatic School in Paris, and singing at the Conservatory. He ran into trouble in both places. In drama school, he was being taught the typical standardized gestures which didn't correspond to what he saw in daily life. He soon left.

At the Conservatory events were far worse. Delsarte wanted nothing more in his life than to be a great singer. Even before he was properly trained, the great composer Hector Berlioz admired his voice and called his powers of expression "unsurpassable." Delsarte took his obvious talent to the Conservatory for training, and there encountered the greatest tragedy of his life. Faulty instruction resulted in the loss of his voice at the age of twenty-three. His career as a singer was finished. But Delsarte himself was only just beginning. He set out to reform the teaching of his time and to find the correct "laws of expression." Laws which would be as exact as mathematical science, and which would not harm those who followed them. In order to do this, he "set out to discover exactly how real people move and speak in every possible emotional circumstance."[3]

The program tells us that Delsarte spent years observing people in hospitals, art galleries, prisons, parks, even studied anatomy at a medical school, all in an attempt to discover how people acted and reacted, not in acting classes, but in real life. He wanted to see how people expressed their feelings of grief, joy, anger, love and fear outside of the theater. And these observations, it says, led him to the answers he was seeking.

We wonder if all this is just the puffery of the program writer, or the story of a true revolutionary. We turn our attention to the man on the podium. Delsarte is speaking: "You can never show truly more than you are capable of experiencing. For the expression of noble emotions, one must feel noble emotions. Imitation will carry you but a short way."[4] "Nothing is more deplorable than a gesture without a motive. External gesture is only the reverberation of internal gesture."[5] "My best results have been attained when I, a passive subject, obeyed an inner inspiration coming from whence I know not and urging me on to results I had not aimed at."[6]

Wow. This man does seem concerned with something other than copying pre-determined gestures and inflections. We look at the date on the program. It is March 20th 1870. Little does anyone here suspect that this man, with the beautiful but weak voice, will be dead in sixteen months. Sitting on the stage behind Delsarte we notice another man. The shadowy figure perhaps? But Delsarte is speaking again: "In a science monthly of last year, I read an interesting account of the hypnotic experiments made by French doctors. A gendarme, on guard in front of the Louvre, was selected for the experiment. Thrown into a mesmeric sleep by means of a few passes, an artist summoned from a neighboring studio, posed him in a model of fear. The unconscious soldier obeyed the artist's hand. But now comes the strangest fact. He felt the emotion, and described himself as experiencing the throes of terror. This seems to bear out an idea…: A perfect reproduction of the outer manifestation of some passion, the giving of the outer sign, will cause a reflex within."[7] "Motion creates emotion."[8]

Wait a minute. He's saying that exterior expressions correspond to and can cause interior emotions. Doesn't this sound familiar? Isn't this what Quintilian and Aaron Hill were saying? Perhaps this man isn't the revolutionary we thought he was. Or, perhaps, there is something to what all these teachers are trying to tell us.

We suddenly remember an idea of the American psychologist William James that "we feel sorry because we cry, angry because we strike, afraid because we tremble, and not that we cry, strike, or tremble, because we are sorry, angry or fearful as the case may be."[9] The physical reaction comes first and then the emotional one. We cannot deny the experience of the soldier in Delsarte's story. By being put in a pose of fear, he began to feel the emotion of fear.

According to this idea, if you see a ferocious bear coming at you, first you run, and then the running causes the fear. We also remember that late in his life, Constantine Stanislavski was thinking along these same lines. Well then, should we go back to our mirror and practice our facial expressions? We are confused. But now Delsarte seems to be backtracking: "...you must bear in mind that the sign is first formed within; so, after all, the exterior expression does not come first...I am treading on egg-shells here, I am conscious."[10]

So, which comes first the physical, or the emotional? The outer, or the inner? Should we work from the outside in, or the inside out? At this point, we're just not sure.

Delsarte is speaking again. He tells us that the first step in studying his ideas is to practice "decomposing" exercises. "These exercises free the channels of expression, and the current of nervous energy can thus rush through them as a stream of water rushes through a channel, unclogged by obstacles."[11] This is something new. This is the first time we've heard anything about relaxation. But as we watch the stage, we see the ghostly figure of Quintilian hovering above Delsarte. Why, we wonder? The answer becomes clear when he speaks again: "I wish you to buy a mirror large enough to reflect your entire figure, and faithfully to practice many hours a day if you wish rapid results."[12] There's that mirror again. Quintilian is smiling.

Delsarte then introduces the man sitting behind him as a Mr. Steele Mackaye of America, and asks him to come forward. We slip into a seat at the back, excited. We're about to get a demonstration.

As Mackaye steps forward, Delsarte explains that there is a universal formula that applies to all things and that that formula is the trinity. For humans the trinity that applies is life, mind and soul. Together, these three principles make up our being. Man communicates these parts of himself in three ways: with the voice, with the gesture, and with the word. He points to Mackaye and explains that the human body itself has three zones: head, torso and limbs. The head is the intellectual center, the torso is the moral center and the limbs the physical center. Each of these centers is further divided into three sub-zones.

Delsarte asks Mackaye to lift one leg. The leg he says has three sections. First is the foot. He asks Mackaye to tap it on the floor. The foot, Delasarte says, represents mental activity. See how a tapping foot shows a person in thought. Next, is the lower leg. This part of the leg is a moral center. He asks Mackaye to kneel. See how kneeling shows reverence, love and obedience. Next, is the upper leg or thigh. This is the physical center of the leg. He asks Mackaye to walk, run and leap. See how physical power comes from this part of the leg.

Delsarte asks Mackaye to stand with both legs wide apart. This, he says, is a position that represents vulgarity, intoxication or fatigue.

He then tells Mackaye to stand with both legs together, with the knees straight and the toes pointed outward. This depicts a condition of feebleness, or of respect. Children and soldiers stand this way.

Next, he asks Mackaye to stand with the strong leg back, its knee straight; the free leg in front, the knee also straight. This position, he tells us, shows, defiance and irritation. He is quick to tell us as a reminder, that these positions are not arbitrary, but are derived from his years of observation of real people. And he warns us that "the artistic idea within must form the outward expression...you cannot mentally plan it at the moment of its execution."[13] He seems to be concerned that people will follow the letter of his teachings and forget the spirit.

Delsarte's Attitudes of the Legs

He thanks Mackaye, who resumes his seat, and tells us that there are also positions for the hand, the arms, the eyes, the lips and jaw, the nose, the upper and lower eyelids, the brows and the mouth. We leave our seat unnoticed, and go back to the lobby.

Delsarte's Attitudes of the Hands

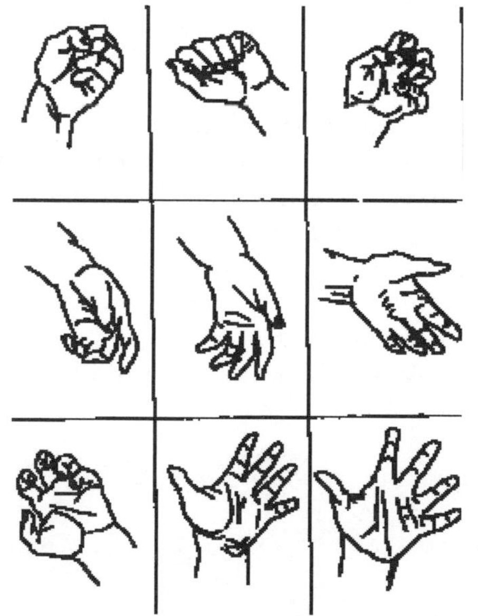

Delsarte. A man ruined by the teaching of his day. A man dedicated to bringing a sense of reality to performing. But we know something he does not. We know that he will die without ever having published anything about his system. And that Steele Mackaye will take America by storm teaching, and in some ways changing, the ideas of Delsarte.

We know that a Delsarte mania will sweep across America and that some will distort his ideas beyond all recognition: "...In the 1890's one finds in magazines advertisements for 'Delsarte corsets,' 'Delsarte cosmetics,' 'Delsarte gowns;' and one manufacturer even advertised a 'Delsarte wooden leg!' "[14] It is one of the great ironies of history that Delsarte acting will come to stand for artificial dramatic poses and declamatory speech. Due to the distortions of others, Delsarte's name will become indelibly associated with a system as confining and false as the one he was trying to overthrow. Luckily, other voices of protest fared better, and as we step through our mirror back to our own time, we leave François Delsarte blissfully unaware of what others will do to his ideas.

Towards the end of the nineteenth century, most actors were still copying their teachers, imitating the outward expressions of emotion, and declaiming their words loudly and beautifully. But great debates about acting raged on. Some felt with Denis Diderot, that an actor should not feel the full emotion of the moment, but... "Learn before a mirror every particle of his despair..."[15] and then distance himself from those passions on stage. Others felt, with Luigi Riccoboni, and Henry Lewes that "The actor...must feel what he acts."[16]

From Quintilian onward, everyone has given their greatest attention to emotions and how to portray them. Yet, great dissatisfaction was fermenting. Perhaps all this focus on emotions was a dead end. Maybe another approach to acting would bear more fruit. We glance at our mirror once again and see the shadowy figure beckoning to us. We do not move. The figure gestures more excitedly. We stay still. The figure stops and regards us. Still, we do not move. The figure sits, and waits.

Chapter 2

The Russian Revolution

We know where the figure wants us to go, and we are afraid. We know that on the other side of that mirror stands the intimidating figure of Constantine Stanislavski; the most important person in the history of acting. Our mind and pulse are racing. How are we to deal with such a giant? How are we to get hold of him? He seems less a human than a monument. Contact with him might uproot every idea we cherish about acting. And we are fearful that if we do not understand his ideas, we will never be real actors.

Will his significance simply wipe us out, obliterate us? Will his brilliance blind us, or worse, will his brilliance make us see ourselves as hopeless phonies? We're just not ready to go through that mirror. We need to catch our breath and calm down. Constantine Stanislavski. The name has become mythological, like Zeus or…wait. The figure is up and smiling and signaling us to step forward through the mirror. Something in his expression convinces us. We go through.

❄

We are in the large bedroom of a young man who is standing before a mirror. If this is Stanislavski, why is he making such ridiculous faces into it? We watch, dumbfounded. The young man continues to observe himself as he makes faces and takes poses. He almost looks like we did when we tried the faces and gestures of Quintilian and Aaron Hill. And if he were not so seriously absorbed in what he was doing, we would burst out laughing.

Suddenly this tall young man begins humming. No, singing. His voice is good, if perhaps a bit hoarse. He continues, in a loud voice, some operatic aria, all the while studying himself in the mirror. After a bit, he stops, looking disappointed and unhappy. He sighs and his eyes droop. It is then that we remember, from his autobiography, *My Life In Art,*[1] that his passionate dream was to become an opera singer, but that his dream was crushed because his voice was simply not good enough. We think of François Delsarte whose hopes to become a classical singer were destroyed by improper vocal training. Despite their differences, we wonder if these two might not share a profound sympathy for each other. Both lost their first artistic loves.

What is it about singing that so moved these men? Some say that singing, at its most basic level, is crying on pitch. And perhaps because singing is such a physical expression of emotion; vibration and breath filling the body, it attracted these passionate men to it. Late in his life, Stanislavski worked with opera singers. If he couldn't be one, he could, at least, be nearby.

But what is this? Stanislavski has left the room and returned with three towels. He wraps one around his waist, one around his chest, and one, like a turban, around his head. He strikes various poses and studies himself in the mirror. As he begins declaiming Shakespearean lines, we realize what he's doing. He's practicing Othello. His gestures are so stilted, his costume so silly, and his movements so bizarre, that we laugh. We are in fact becoming hysterical. This great god is prancing around in towels, making faces in a mirror and speaking in the most affected manner imaginable.

It soothes us a little to realize that this great man did not spring from the womb fully formed, knowing all the right answers, but that he, like us, struggled and stumbled. In fact, at first, he did almost everything wrong.

The first time Stanislavski appeared on a stage he was a small child, and managed to burn down the set. This event foreshadowed the very different way in which he would set the theater on fire in his later life.

As a young man, Stanislavski was smitten by anything that smacked of the theatrical. As the son of a sympathetic and well to do merchant in Moscow, he had the opportunity to attend many circus, ballet, opera, theater and musical performances. And these fired his imagination. He tried to imitate whatever he saw. At his house he put on circus performances using friends and relatives. They used make-up and props and copied routines they had seen. Eventually they realized that without elaborate sets, costumes and props, they could never achieve the level of production for which they longed. So, Stanislavski hit upon a particularly creative idea. A puppet theater required only miniature furniture pieces, and miniature costumes, and these they could make. A Stanislavski marionette theater was born. This enterprise was run like a real theater, with the performers charging admission and issuing tickets. Perhaps somewhere inside, Stanislavski knew he was practicing his future.

When a new wing was added to their house, Stanislavski's father did an extraordinary thing. He included in it, a theatrical playing space and an area for backstage dressing rooms. Imagine this level of support. The young Constantine Stanislavski was provided an area which could be used as a small theater in his own house! The marionettes were forgotten. This space was for real people, and Stanislavski seized the opportunity. He appointed himself the director of this home theater and chose the plays to be performed in it. And, of course, he acted in it. But how did he act in those early years? Was he brilliant, a genius? Hardly. He began, like so many of us, by imitating his favorite actors.

Stanislavski especially loved a comedic actor he saw many times at The Imperial Little Theater, who moved his face in funny ways. So Stanislavski tried to do the same, but his performance fell flat. He wasn't the great success he'd hoped to be. The best comment he received was that his performance was, "rather nice."[2]

The young actor was crestfallen. He'd imitated his favorite actor pretty well he thought, so why hadn't it worked? What was wrong? He didn't have an answer, but something more important was beginning. This questioning, this search for excellence, would occupy him for the rest of his life, and lead him to his greatest achievements.

But since he didn't know what else to do, the young actor continued to copy actors he admired. He felt dissatisfied, knowing something essential was missing, but went on nonetheless.

Why? He loved the attention and the power he felt on stage. And who's to blame him? How many of us have done the same? We step onto the stage, inadequately prepared, scared to death, wanting to run, but go on anyway hoping a lightning strike of inspiration will hit and make us brilliant. And when it's time for the curtain call, we will bask in the applause and the praise, and bow humbly. It's a great dream. Unfortunately, it rarely comes true. Mostly we are left with a vague sense of uneasiness. The praise is never enough, and if it is, we feel we really don't deserve it. And so, we move on to the next production hoping it will be the one. Hoping everything will work and that the praise will be deserved. This is what Stanislavski did. And his journey was a painful one. If he was going to continue copying others, who were his models to be? What kind of acting did Stanislavski see around him?

The great Russian serf actor Michael Shchepkin described the usual acting style of the time this way, "...the playing of the actors was considered excellent when none of them spoke in his natural voice, when they declaimed their lines in a completely artificial manner...and when each word was accompanied by a gesture. The words 'love,' 'passion,' 'treason,' were uttered as loud as possible, ...And when, for example, the actor finished a long monologue at the moment of leaving the stage, he had to go off into the wings with his right arm raised."[3] This is largely what Stanislavski saw around him.

But he was also aware of something different, something deeper. He knew of Shchepkin and that he'd written, "It is not important that you play well or ill; it is important that you play truthfully."[4] But though this precept was of great importance to Stanislavski, he never had the chance to see Shchepkin put it into practice because in 1863, the very year of Stanislavski's birth, Shchepkin, after fifty-seven years in the theater, died. Shchepkin had striven his entire life to present living, breathing human beings upon the stage, but, unfortunately, left no guide book, no map that could show others how to do the same.

The great question remained: How does one combine the need to pretend, with the need to express something true? And the answer continued to elude the young Stanislavski.

For years Stanislavski went on trying anything and everything to achieve greatness as an actor. He studied his posture, facial expressions and gestures in a mirror. He then would go on stage attempting to copy what he thought had been successful there. But he still spoke too fast, dropped the ends of his words, gestured wildly, forced emotion, and always, always felt tense. In one case, he was so out of control that he cut a fellow actor with a prop dagger.

He tried, to the best of his ability, to correct all of these faults. For years he thought the answers lay in externals. He sought solutions to his acting problems in costumes, in makeup, in props. He tried different facial expressions, different voices, different walks. He performed everywhere he could and sometimes met with success and sometimes with failure. The failures haunted him and the successes gave only the briefest pleasure because they were accidental.

But he pushed on. He even performed in a theater of dubious reputation. The play was a risqué French farce and he was so embarrassed to be seen in it, that he changed his name so as not to be recognized. Yes, Stanislavski is his stage name, not his real one. He was born Constantine Alexeiev, but for the play in question, took the name of a retired Polish actor, Stanislavski, for his own. But when he stepped onto the stage, he recognized, in the audience, his father, his mother, and the governesses of his sisters. He was mortified. But still, he went on. He continued to experiment. He tried memorizing words mechanically so that he could say them at any speed. He took ballet classes. He studied opera. But even when he met with success, he felt false on stage, that he was "engaged in evil work."[5] So, at age twenty-one, with more than twenty shows behind him, Constantine Stanislavski entered the Imperial Dramatic School of Moscow. But after a scant three weeks of classes, he was gone. A drama school dropout.

Why? It was more than that the teachers wanted the students to copy them. And it was more than that the teachers wanted results without ever teaching the students how to achieve them. It was even more than the fact that there was no practical step-by-step program to follow. No, it was the soul shattering feeling that "I would be deprived of my own individuality, bad as it was."[6]

Yes, one's uniqueness. From Quintilian to Aaron Hill through Delsarte to the Imperial Dramatic School, conformity to the rules was the highest good. Even when great individual actors emerged, like David Garrick, acting theorists tried to make their individuality into a new set of rules for all to follow. Differences in these systems came down to execution. If your gesture was smoother, your voice louder, your postures and movements more graceful, you were the better actor.

But Stanislavski wanted to be true to himself and not be a copy of his teacher, who was a copy of his teacher, who was a copy of his teacher...and so on. It is a terrifying feeling to lose one's self, one's "specialness" just so that one can be re-formed with a cookie cutter. Stanislavski felt that actors were being stamped from a pre-made stencil and sent out into the acting world, and he rebelled against it. And so, like Delsarte, he set out to discover for himself the answers to the questions that burned so deeply inside of him.

But the road ahead was hard. He met with some success and much failure. His inability to find a reliable technique tortured him. He became so desperate to find the core of one character, that he persuaded some friends to lock him in the cellar of a French castle so that the proper feeling of his part might come to him. For two hours he stayed inside this dark and damp cellar trying to repeat his lines with the appropriate emotion. But all he succeeded in doing was coming down with a cold.[7] The answers he sought were clearly not to be found in this way.

But little by little, Stanislavski began to understand some important things. By working with a professional company, he learned the value of discipline, of arriving on time and rehearsing with concentration and focus. From a professional actress, he learned to look into the eyes of, and really see, his fellow actor. He learned how to stand still on the stage, and how to show restraint in the expression of emotion.

Through directing he learned that each actor has an important function in the overall scheme of a play. He took to heart the saying of Shchepkin that "there are no small parts, only small actors." He began to see the value of painting characters in more than black and white colors. He saw that: "When you play an evil man look to see where he is good. When you play an old man, look to see where he is young."[8]

He realized that while external acting could not bring him to the style of acting he sought, "it helped prepare the soil for it."[9] And perhaps most importantly of all, he understood that there is "an unbreakable bond between physical and psychical nature."[10] The mind-body connection that Delsarte spoke of was clear and crucial to Stanislavski. But he still did not know how to consistently activate that connection, and so, felt that his successes were largely the result of lucky accidents.

But what's this? Stanislavski has left the bedroom. In fact, he has been gone for some time, and the figure in the mirror is impatiently waving us forward. We need little prompting and step through.

❄

We find ourselves standing just outside a large restaurant called The Slavic Bazaar, in Moscow. A nearby newspaper tells us that the date is June 22, 1897. We step inside the restaurant and stand behind two men who seem to be waiting for a table. The maitre d' addresses the tall broad man as Mr. Stanislavski and tells him that the private room is ready. We realize that the forty year old man with him is the playwright and teacher Vladimir Nemirovich-Danchenko, and as the maitre d' leads them, we follow. No one seems to notice. The two begin talking excitedly, and we soon realize that we are witnessing the creation of the most important and influential theater of the twentieth century, the Moscow Art Theater.

Stanislavski and Danchenko are discussing what they feel is wrong with the Russian theater. They feel that rehearsal time is too short, that actors have little discipline, that productions are unoriginal with false acting and cardboard scenery, and that the plays being performed are poor in quality.[11] Next, they discuss who should be in their company. They carefully go over every actor who might be a possibility, and argue about whether this one or that one is worth considering. They are both very passionate, and we get so caught up in their enthusiasm that we almost start suggesting some actors we know. Well, they wouldn't hear us if we did, anyway. They discuss everything. They decide that every actor should have a dressing room of his or her own, that the greenrooms should have in them a library, pianos and chess boards, and that no one should enter a greenroom in a coat or hat,[12] they even discuss the price of tickets.

After many hours of such detailed talk, the two men come to a crucial topic. The division of power. When it is suggested that Danchenko be in charge of what plays should be chosen for performance, Stanislavski puts up little resistance. He seems to respect Danchenko's superiority in this area. But when the subject of the artistic control of the productions themselves comes up, a tension begins to build. We step closer to their table. There is a tense silence. When Stanislavski begins to speak, it is with great passion. He feels that the production of the plays, and that the work of the actors and the director should be under his control. Danchenko is silent. Stanislavski is relentless. He argues that he has fifteen years of practical experience in these matters and that it is only logical that he should be in charge of them. Danchenko is disturbed by this. Too much power will reside with Stanislavski. He expresses his uneasiness. Stanislavski insists, with tremendous energy, that his control of all the artistic aspects of production is crucial to the future success of their theater. Again, he invokes his experience as a director and actor and doesn't seem to notice the discomfort of his partner. Or maybe he does, and presses on because he wants what he wants. The two men are at an impasse.

Stanislavski's stubbornness is surprising. We know he has been wracked with doubts about his abilities and yet, here he is demanding the right to control all artistic decisions having to do with staging, acting and directing. Something unconscious is driving him, and is threatening the very enterprise he is hoping to create. This is his dream. He is on the verge of leaving the amateur world and entering the professional one, yet he is standing in his own way.

Luckily, the birth of this theater is not to be denied. They agree to a compromise. Stanislavski may propose plays for the theater to produce, but Danchenko will have the ultimate say. For his part, Danchenko may make suggestions with regard to the artistic presentation of the repertoire, but Stanislavski will have the final word. This mutual veto power settles the issue, and the two men continue working out both the ideals and the details of their dream. When they finish, eighteen hours later, the groundwork for the Moscow Art Theater has been laid.

As we watch these men, we become inspired. Haven't we too wanted to start a theater based on our pure love of drama? Haven't we, in fact, had long and heated artistic discussions with our theatrical soul-mates that lasted late into the night ending with passionate agreement to start a theater? And weren't those nights some of the best we ever had? And the next day, didn't the idea of a theater of our own seem daunting and far away? Of course. But these men had the means and the dedication to take the astounding step of making talk, real.

We watch these men, and know the future. We know that the doors of the MAT (Moscow Art Theater) will open October 14, 1898 with a production of the play *Tsar Fyodor,* and that the reaction will be favorable. The production is original, the scenery more detailed and realistic than Moscow audiences are used to, and the acting more believable than the norm. Stanislavski and Danchenko will succeed in just the way they hope. Their theater will set a higher standard and everyone will know it.

But their joy will be short-lived. The next four productions fail and the fledgling theater will be near collapse. The next production they mount must succeed or the MAT will be extinct.

We look over at Danchenko and know that it is his literary taste that will save the theater. It is he who will see the value of a play called *The Seagull* by the famous short story writer, Anton Chekhov. And it is the production of that play which will ensure the success of the MAT. Amazingly, Stanislavski will be so puzzled by Chekhov's work that he will ask Danchenko "Are you sure it can be performed at all? I just can't make head or tail of it."[13] Danchenko has not only to convince Stanislavski to direct the play, but must also talk Chekhov into granting the MAT the right to present it. It is Danchenko who will see what is revolutionary about Chekhov's creation, not Stanislavski. Danchenko sees that the portrayal of everyday life in the play hides the deep desires of the characters and that the unspoken communication between these characters carries much of the play's power.

We know that Danchenko will rehearse the play more than Stanislavski and that at its opening on December 17, 1898, they will experience an unprecedented success. So important will this play become to the MAT, that they will have the image of a seagull permanently painted onto the theater's front curtain.

In the next six years, the MAT will present twenty productions, four of them by Chekhov. The theater will also produce plays from writers as diverse as Ibsen, Shakespeare and the Symbolist poet, Maurice Maeterlinck. The reputation of the theater and its achievements will travel through Europe and America making it the most talked about company in the world. People will speak of the realism of the sets, the use of offstage sounds such as birds and distant storms to create atmosphere, the ensemble acting and the overall brilliance of the direction. "Chekhov unintentionally gave the MAT the key to a new performance style: psychological realism. Here the hidden communication and conflicts between all classes and types of people—so imbedded in our normal daily experiences that we hardly notice them—were exposed."[14]

And yet there were problems. For one, Chekhov disliked Stanislavski's direction of his plays. More than that, he abhorred Stanislavski's portrayal of Trigorin in *The Seagull.* He complained that his plays were comedies and not the serious tragedies of the

Russian people into which Stanislavski turned them. For another, some accused the theater of "Naturalism." That is, they felt the MAT was only interested in presenting the behavioral details of ordinary life. But while Stanislavski was interested in what he called inner truth, he was never in favor of naturalism on the stage.

But these criticisms were as nothing compared to the deeper problems that concerned Stanislavski. He noticed that his actors were erratic. Some nights they were inspired and some nights they were stale. And while they took classes in fencing, dancing, singing, and gymnastics, they still lacked a technique for creating the inner life of a character. But what shook Stanislavski to his core, was his own acting. He felt dead on stage. He found himself acting mechanically and with little or no inner feeling. He was empty and drained and could no longer "feel" his roles. He was acting from muscle memory alone. This frightened him as nothing else ever had. And after an exhausting but triumphant tour of Germany in 1906, Stanislavski left the company to rethink everything.

Danchenko and Stanislavski are now leaving the Slavic Bazaar and we follow them. Outside the restaurant, we notice the figure from the mirror reflected in the café window. He is waving us toward him. We watch the two creators of the Moscow Art Theater hurriedly cross the street still talking out the details of their creation, and at that second, a profound admiration for these two dreamers sweeps over us. After a moment, we turn away, and step through the window.

❄

We are in a place of astonishing beauty. The climate is mild, and below the cliff on which we stand, is the deep blue Baltic Sea. Sitting on a bench nearby is the forty-three year old Constantine Stanislavski. He gazes out at the sea but does not seem to see it. We realize that we are in Finland in the year of 1906. It is here that Stanislavski has come to rethink his whole approach to the art of acting. He has by his side, a notebook. It is the journal he has been keeping since 1889 of his thoughts and discoveries about acting. But he is not looking at it. He seems far away. He is in fact, reviewing in his mind the past twenty-five years of his life in the theater. How is it possible for

Tommaso Salvini to play Othello for so many years and still present it freshly, he wonders? Why is the great Italian actress Eleanora Duse able to do the same? Why can't he? These questions torment him.

Below him, he notices waves crashing against hard and jagged rocks. The water and the land are fighting each other. But further down the beach, where there are no rocks, the tide smoothly blankets the sand. Stanislavski takes note. How can he create a receptive state of mind that will allow the waves of inspiration to wash over him? How can an actor create a state of mind that will invite inspiration to him, and not, like the rocks, block its path? He has sought the answer in props, costumes, voices, walks and other means of external expression. But these devices ultimately have failed him.

As he considers the great actors he has seen, he comes to a startling insight. What they all have in common, he realizes, is a lack of tension on stage. There is simply no bodily strain. Even in moments of high emotion, these actors never show any extraneous tension. Obviously, these actors place great value on *relaxation.* Stanislavski himself, even after all these years, has never cured himself of nervousness and strain on stage. What if he could? Would relaxation create a lure for inspiration? He picks up his notebook and writes. He is on to something important and he knows it.

Stanislavski will spend months writing down more of his insights and the next three years trying them out in his own acting. He will realize the power of *concentration* when it is centered on the stage and not in the auditorium. He has, he realizes, often found his attention leaving the stage and wandering out toward the audience. In truth, so have we.

We are struck by the similarities with Delsarte and Hill. Delsarte too thought relaxation of paramount importance, devising "decomposing" exercises to achieve it. Hill, we remember, said, "...whenever you can forget an audience, you will charm them." Stanislavski is not the only one who has been on this path.

What separates him from the others, however, is his relentless quest for truth in acting, and his drive to codify a method to achieve that truth. For Stanislavski, it is the other line in Keats's *Ode On A Grecian Urn* that stands as his motto: Truth is beauty. He has turned the aesthetic rallying cry of the 18th century, that beauty is truth, upside down. It is not that whatever achieves beauty is automatically truthful, but rather, that whatever achieves truthfulness is automatically beautiful.

We are again amazed at the tenacity of this man. We know that in the three years during which he will experiment with his new-found ideas, he will actually get worse as an actor. We know that the members of his company will dismiss his ideas as misguided and foolish. But we also know that Stanislavski will push on. In 1909 he will post a notice at the MAT announcing that rehearsals for Turgenev's *A Month In The Country* will be conducted in a new way. One can almost hear the moans of the company right now. But when that production opens, Stanislavski will have many converts. He will finally succeed in creating and transmitting a method that gives actors a pathway to inspiration on stage, and one that can be taught on a step-by-step basis. His years of struggle, disappointment, searching and digging will finally yield some nuggets of the purest gold.

Stanislavski stands, stretches and strolls along the cliff side. We follow. But in order not to run into him, we step too near the edge, and find ourselves falling towards the rocks below.

❄

We land on a hardwood floor.

We shake our head and try to recover our senses. We seem to be in a dance studio. There is a mirror along one wall and a barre running along its length. Strewn randomly around the floor of the studio are banners and flags. We turn some over and read what they say: RELAXATION, CONCENTRATION, GIVEN CIRCUMSTANCES, ACTION.

These are the words on some of the flags, and there are many more. This, we realize, is THE SYSTEM! Spread out before us, is the fruit of Stanislavski's many years of struggle. We feel giddy and throw a handful of flags into the air as if we'd found a pirate treasure of gold doubloons. Then we see a startling thing. Stepping from the mirror onto the hardwood floor, is the FIGURE itself, our guide.

We freeze. The figure coming through the mirror is wearing a long tunic, impossibly high sandals, and a mask featuring a jutting chin and mouth hole. He stands over seven feet high. We want to run, but cannot. Slowly, the figure raises its arms and removes its mask. It is a man with long dark hair and a smile on his face.

"I am Thespis," he announces. "Do not think your journey is finished because I now appear before you. I only reveal myself to help you understand this great man's contribution to our art. From here, there are still many places to go."

Thespis. The first actor of the western world. He has been taking us on this journey from place to place and from teacher to teacher.

He picks up the banner marked, RELAXATION, and speaks. Tension, he tells us, is our greatest enemy. It pinches the voice, stiffens the muscles, shortens the breath and blocks the mind. When you are totally tense, you cannot move, speak, or think. And yet nothing, he explains, is more impossible than to command someone to RELAX. We understand this, having been commanded to do this many times and feeling only self conscious in response.

One way to approach relaxation, Thespis tells us, is through its opposite, tension. He asks us to stand. We do. He wants us to tense our whole body, tighten every muscle. We do. After a brief moment, he tells us to release all the tension. Again, we do. What relief! Our muscles do feel as though they've let go a bit.

Now, Thespis asks us to tense just the right side of our body, leaving the left side relaxed. We try this, but find tension unconsciously creeping over to the left part of our body. See, he tells us, if we are not made aware of our tenseness, it can quietly take control of our bodies. We see his point. He now asks us to stand straight with only the tension necessary to keep us upright. As we do this, we wonder at our situation. A long dead Ancient Greek is explaining the work of a Russian actor-teacher-director of the early twentieth century. Where, in fact, is Stanislavski, we ask. Why isn't he telling us all this? Thespis answers: "At this moment, Constantine Stanislavski is busy changing his System."

Oh.

He again tells us to stand straight. We do. From this position, Thespis asks us to drop our head slowly and bend forward. He tells us to try and feel each of the vertebrae in our backs separately. He wants us to feel each one loosening, letting go. When we are fully over, he tells us to come slowly back up, vertebra by vertebra. When we are up again, we feel less tension in our bodies.

Thespis tells us that yoga and breathing exercises also help to reduce bodily tension. But some tension, he explains, is required when one performs, otherwise one might not be able to stand up. We cannot perform without enormous amounts of energy. So the total elimination of tension is not the goal. What we aim for is the reduction of unnecessary strain. This, he explains, leaves the channels of emotional expression open. Tension, of course, will squeeze them off.

But it is not enough to practice relaxation exercises in isolation. It is best, Thespis tells us, to relax parts of the body during performance, to be aware of body tension as you are acting, and reduce unnecessary strain right on stage. This is possible because of the dual nature of the actor. Thespis explains that Stanislavski speaks of two presences on the stage at one time. There is the actor, and the character.

We are surprised by this, because we have always thought that Stanislavski stood for the total merging of the player and the part. Thespis says that we are mistaken. Stanislavski is a practical man of the theater and knows that while the character must use the actor, they must not truly become as one. Becoming conscious of tension in our bodies takes practice, says Thespis, and that is why we do relaxation exercises. Again, we think of Delsarte and his decomposing exercises.

Thespis turns over three other flags. They read, MIND, WILL, and EMOTION. These, he explains, are the three parts of the actor that Stanislavski considered the pillars of his inner landscape. If the actor's mind, his will and his feelings are all engaged, he will come alive. Stanislavski's system is meant to occupy the mind, motivate the will and release the emotional life of the actor. The mind is the most easily approached of these three, while the emotions are the most fickle. We cannot help but think again of Delsarte and his three-part division of the actor into life, mind and soul.

"Disaster,"Thespis says, "has struck many an actor who has tried to force an emotion through his system. Emotion is not subject to command. Just ask someone to cry, and watch what happens."

"Emotion," Thespis tells us, "must be coaxed out of hiding, not directly accosted. If we reach for it, it will run away. But if we concentrate on something else, something that magnetizes our mind and will, it may come along with us. All of the techniques that Stanislavski discovered are directed at one or all of these three aspects of the actor."

Relaxation, I suggest, is most important for freeing the mind. Thespis agrees.

Next, he picks up a flag that says, CONCENTRATION. "On the stage," Thespis says, "actors are always concentrating on something. Unfortunately, this concentration may be on their nervousness, or on the audience, and this draws the actor away from his true purpose. Therefore, actors must be trained to force their attention onto the stage and its reality." But how, we wonder?

"Your shoe is untied," says Thespis and points to my feet. I look down and see that my right shoe lace is loose and bend down to fix it. When I look up, Thespis is again wearing his mask.

"Did you notice me putting it on?" No, I confess, I didn't. I apologize to him for not paying attention. "That's a good phrase, 'paying attention,'" he says. "Indeed you will pay a high price if attention is wrongly placed. And you will be greatly repaid if it is rightly placed. You shouldn't apologize to me, your attention was correctly centered on what you were doing, on your shoe and its lace. You see, the distraction of the audience disappears when your mind is occupied with something else. Stanislavski realized this simple but profound truth."

Thespis takes off his mask and places it on the floor in front of us. A little further away he places a large glowing golden ball. He asks us to study the mask. We observe its shape and the materials from which it appears to be made. We pick it up in order to assess its weight and we hold it up to our face. We feel its texture and smell its scent. We tap it to see what sound it makes. Thespis asks us if we have been aware of the glowing ball. No, we say, we have forgotten about it. Good, he says. Stanislavski speaks of a "circle of attention"[15], Thespis tells us, and we have been absorbed by the closest object in that circle.

What is the object of your attention right now, he asks. You are, we reply. "Correct. Your concentration shifted to me when I began to explain. This constant shifting of attention is crucial to living on the stage."

"If you are ever without a proper *object of attention,* then you are empty. And any emptiness on stage will be filled up with either dead moments or clichéd ones." We recognize the truth of this. There have been moments on stage when we weren't sure where to look or what to do, and in those moments we felt a growing panic that we hoped went unnoticed. If we'd known what the object of attention was in those seconds, we would have felt safer and less self-conscious. As we are thinking these thoughts, our eyes shift from Thespis, to the mask in our hands, to Thespis's hand as we give his mask back to him, to Thespis's eyes, to the mask again, and then to our shoes. A continuous and logical stream of objects has seized our concentration.

In life, we realize, we do this object shifting all the time. When we are waiting in a doctor's office, even before we sit, our eyes sweep the table tops and magazine racks for something to occupy our minds. When we sit, we take in the chair before we lower ourselves, we glance around the room to look at the people, we look at the cover of our magazine. We are constantly concentrating, and we are constantly shifting our concentration. Even when we are daydreaming, we are concentrating on some inner thought or feeling.

"When you lose your concentration on the stage," Thespis suddenly says, "you can often regain it by focusing on the closest object. And by 'object,' I include people. Further, you must realize that not all objects of attention are of equal importance. In what you call 'a doctor's office,' your attention will be more engaged by the doctor when he or she comes to get you than by the other people in the room. When you play a part, you must develop a sense of proportion regarding which points of attention are important and which are less so. This circle of attention helps you to really 'see' the stage and the others on it. Now, let's put relaxation and concentration together." Thespis asks us to step over to the golden ball.

As we do so, we realize that he can read our thoughts. How else could he have known about the doctor's office?

Thespis asks us to stand directly over the ball, and to stretch our arms as high over our heads as we can. He tells us to imagine that we are trying to reach a book on a high shelf, but that it is just out of reach. He tells us to slowly drop our arms beginning first with the wrists, then the forearms to the elbow, and then to drop the upper arms at the shoulders Our arms are now completely down. He tells us to drop our head.

Thespis explains that we are going to go down slowly through our spine, as we did before, but that this time we will use the glowing golden ball as an object for our attention.

When we do this, it feels different. We have a goal this time. The ball captures our interest, and so we have a reason for bending down to get a closer look at it. We are excited to be so close to this magical glowing ball. It seems to be radiating a pleasant warmth that makes us feel good.

"You see," he says, "you are having feelings even though I did not ask you for any." It's true. We were not focused on having any particular feelings. We were focused on examining the fascinating object before us. "Did you think about me?" asks Thespis. No, we did not. "It was as if you were alone with the ball, wasn't it?" Yes, we reply. This feeling, of being alone when others are around, Stanislavski calls

"Public Solitude,"[16] Thespis explains. He picks up one of the banners from the floor and that is just what it says; PUBLIC SOLITUDE.

Sometimes, on stage, we have felt this. It is a strange and wonderful feeling to act as if only the people and the furniture on the stage are present, to forget about that huge space where the audience is sitting. Yet, if one really acted like this, we wonder, wouldn't one speak as though in one's own living room? How could the audience hear you if you are truly acting private in public? "Make no mistake," thunders Thespis, "Stanislavski believes that a clear and powerful voice is a necessity for an actor. Simply put, you MUST BE HEARD AND UNDERSTOOD! It takes practice to create public solitude and still be heard by the audience. This is one of the main reasons why the actor studies voice. You'll learn more about that later, however."

So far, we've learned that concentrating on objects of attention creates a state of public solitude, and that this state helps to keep us from falling into the clichéd behavior we think the audience expects. Thespis tells us that there are many ways to deepen our ability to concentrate. One way, is to study an object for a certain period of time, say three minutes, and then to describe everything we can remember about it. We can give histories to an object; when we last used it, when we first used it, our emotional associations with it. Another exercise designed to increase our powers of concentration, he tells us, is to multiply numbers in our head, while others ask us questions.[17]

Concentration, he tells us, does not mean just squinting our eyes and staring at something. Concentration is not a frozen thing, but requires an alive and active mind. When we concentrate on something, we are *doing* something. We are assessing, judging, weighing, reacting to the object of our attention. This reminder helps us. We have been guilty, when asked to CONCENTRATE, of simply staring harder, furrowing our brows and tensing our jaw. We've put on the look of concentration, but not actively concentrated.

Thespis turns over a card that says, SENSORY RECALL. This he tells us, is a part of concentration. A useful concentration exercise is to recall the events of a day using the five senses. Try to recall waking up this morning, he tells us. What did the air feel like on your skin? What was the weight of the sheet or blanket like? What texture did you feel against your body? What did the room smell like? What was the temperature? Was it cold? Cool? Warm? Hot? What sounds did you hear as you arose? What was the taste in your mouth? What woke you? What did you first see when you awakened? When you got out of bed was the floor cold, soft, warm? Was the surface wooden or carpeted? When did the demands and tasks of the day hit you? Recall any part of your day in this way, and your powers of concentration will increase, he says.

In addition, he adds, you can go deeper. "Recall another part of your day, the objects and people you see. Remember to use all five senses when you do this recall. But when you do it this time, include your reactions to everything. If you heard a church bell, remember how it made you feel. If you smelled food, remember if you wanted it or were put off by it. Associate *sense memories* with feelings and judgments and you will prepare the ground for emotional arousal."

Thespis turns over another banner and affixes it to the wall. It reads, IMAGINATION. Without this, Thespis announces, you cannot act. How can you create something that does not exist if you do not use your imagination, he asks. "Whatever character you play does not truly exist until YOU create it. That is an act of the imagination."

"Look at the golden ball," he commands. We do. "Imagine that it is an egg and that inside it, is growing a poisonous serpent. Imagine further, that the serpent is about to hatch." We do. "Good. Now, pick it up." We look at Thespis, and down at the ball. We don't know anything about this Thespis. Only that he is possessed of powers that enable him to travel through time and space. We don't know his heart, his intentions. Suppose there *is* a snake in that ball, and that to illustrate some point, he allows it to bite us? This whole thing is getting a little crazy. We do not move toward the ball.

"You do not trust me?" asks Thespis. No, we quite firmly reply. "Well then," he goes on, "suppose that the ball is not an egg and that there is no serpent. Imagine instead, that inside that glowing golden ball is your talent. That precious and mysterious essence that makes you special and unique. And imagine further, that if you pick it up and place it inside you, it will always guide and bless you. And that if you are true to it, it will be true to you. Now, will you pick it up?"

As Thespis has been speaking, we have been staring at the ball. It has changed several times from a dangerous egg, to a precious gift. Back and forth the thing has shifted. When we think of it as an egg we are repelled by it, but when we think of it as the container of our talent, we are attracted to it. Again, we do not move. We do not know what to believe.

"The truth is," says Thespis, "that the ball is whatever your imagination makes it. Just as it is possible for you to become whatever your imagination makes you. Imagination is limitless and is one of our most powerful tools. It enlivens the mind, the will and the emotions. Just now, many feelings went through you. But I never said to feel anything. I only engaged your imagination by using images, and these images allowed your emotions to flow." The truth of this is unmistakable. "And, when the ball held your talent, you wanted to go to it. Your will pulled you forward, but your judgment held you still." Again, the truth of this is undeniable.

"But what did I do that helped you to believe in the images I presented to you?" asks Thespis. We have no reply. "Just now, with the ball, how did I do it?" We're still not sure. We're more than a little intimidated by this figure. We do wish he'd take off those huge shoes that make him tower over us. Thespis smiles. He bends down and begins to remove his shoes. "You need to develop a sense of how we accomplish what we do. It is important to think in this way without my presence. After a while, I will become a figure inside of you and not outside." He has both shoes off now, and stands smiling before us. "Better?" he asks. Much, we reply.

He picks up another banner and holds it up. It says, MAGIC IF. This, he tells us is what allowed us to believe in the images of the ball and the egg. "Instead of 'if,' I said 'suppose' but it means the same thing. Stanislavski says that the word 'if' is the key that opens the door to the imagination. When I first told you that the ball was an egg containing a poisonous serpent, you acted toward it *as if* what I told you was a fact. You see, that 'if' catapults you into the world of the imagination. The word 'if' is magical in that it gives us permission to be something other than we are. It enables us to place ourselves in situations in which we have never been, and to live in those situations."

"Now imagine that you had known that the ball was not an egg. The simple word 'if' would still allow you to act toward the ball as if it were an egg. 'If' allows you to modulate from the key of reality into the new key of the imagination without violating your *sense of truth.* 'If' can put us anywhere; past, present, future, Earth, Mars, or in a bottle. It can make us anything; person, object, animal, alien, warrior, philosopher or even Ancient Greek. We must use it, if we are to deal successfully with what is on the next banner."

Thespis picks up another flag. It reads, CIRCUMSTANCES. "Your imagination, activated by the magic 'if,' is what enables you to enter the imaginary circumstances of a play."

"You are not Hamlet," Thespis states matter-of-factly. We certainly agree. "But if you were Hamlet, what would it be like? In order to answer that question, you would need to understand Hamlet's circumstances. If you were a thirty-year-old Prince of Denmark given to studying the eternal issues of mankind, and you returned home only to discover that your uncle had murdered your father and that your mother had married that very same uncle, how would you feel? Don't answer yet, just sit down and close your eyes."

We sit cross-legged on the studio floor and close our eyes. After a few moments Thespis speaks in a quiet voice.

"You are approaching the castle. It is dark out and your horse is galloping over muddy ground. You are being splattered but do not care. You are desperate to get home for your father's funeral. Your father. To you he always seemed the very definition of a man. You always wondered if you could measure up. The castle looms ahead of you. It appears to be like a huge coffin inside of which everything is dead. You shake off this morbid image and press on. Why think such thoughts? You will be king now, unless rumors of your mother's marriage to your uncle prove true. But how could she marry anyone without a proper period of mourning? She wouldn't. She will respect the memory of her husband, your father. You reach back to feel the pack that holds your black clothes of mourning. Yes, it's still there.

Do you even want to be king? There will, of course, be great power, but your life will never be yours again. You are now close enough to see the silhouetted guards on the battlements. At least, you think, the sunlight that is Ophelia is inside. The drawbridge lowers and the castle swallows you up.

Attendants rush towards you as you dismount. They greet you and bow. You are glad to see some of them for you have known them all your life. They all offer words of comfort concerning the death of King Hamlet, but are tense when they explain that not only have you missed your father's funeral, but that the marriage of your mother and uncle is only a few weeks away. You stand stunned. It begins to rain. You do not move, and then, in a daze, you reach into your pack and take out your mourning clothes. Standing in the rain, before your attendants, you strip off your riding clothes and don your suit of solemn black. And as they watch, you walk slowly into the castle." Thespis takes a breath and asks, "are you there?"

We are. We keep our eyes closed, seeing the scene and feeling saddened and enraged.

"Your inner feelings are aroused by the circumstances I have painted, are they not?" We nod our head. "According to Stanislavski, the key to acting is to apply your inner life to the circumstances of the character. In this way, you do not just play yourself, you *use* yourself in the service of the part. If you are absent, the part will be lifeless. But if *only* you are present, the character will disappear."

"Notice also, that when your mind was engaged with the circumstances, which your imagination allowed you to enter, you were both relaxed and concentrated. All the elements we've talked about so far combined to create vivid sensory images which stimulated your emotions. Now, after hearing and imagining the story I have just told you, aren't you just itching to DO something?"

Yes, we reply. Our body is all revved up with no place to go. We're excited. Energy is flowing through us and we want to move.

"Not yet," says Thespis. "Stay still. I want to make another point."

We try to stay put, but notice that our foot is shaking rapidly back and forth.

"Suppose you must act the following short two-person scene:"

A: Hi, how are you?
B: Fine.
A: What happened today?
B: Nothing much. You?
A: Nothing. Want some? *(Offering a drink.)*
B: No thanks.
A: Jenny?
B: Yes?
A: Nothing.

"Without a circumstance, such a scene would be flat and uninteresting. But if we add even a simple circumstance to it, it will come alive. Suppose we say that characters "A" and "B" are boyfriend and girlfriend. And let us further suppose that this scene takes place in the apartment they share. And finally, let us add to the circumstance that "B" has just found out that her boyfriend "A" has been having an affair with her best friend. With these simple circumstances, the scene will change. It will have a very specific life and dynamic. It will no longer be boring, and yet we never changed the words. All we did, was to give it a circumstance.

Suppose that we change the circumstances again. This time let us imagine that character "A" has decided to kill character "B." And let us further suppose that the instrument of murder will be a poison drink. Let's try it."

From out of nothing, Thespis produces a table, two chairs, and a cup. He sits in one of the chairs and waves me over. Yes, we are about to play a scene with Thespis.

"You are character 'A,'" he announces, "And you may change the name 'Jenny,' to 'Thespis.'" He snatches a newspaper out of the air and begins reading it. A strange sight indeed; an ancient Greek reading a newspaper. We realize that we must enter, and that we must enter from somewhere. This makes us wonder where we might have been. Perhaps at school, and perhaps Thespis is our abusive father. We realize we are creating "circumstances." Now, since we don't want "dad" to be suspicious, we enter cheerfully.

US: Hi, how are you. *(We sit, wiping our brow like it's a hot day outside.)*

THESPIS: Fine. *(Thespis kind of snaps this word out, like we're interrupting him.)*

US: What happened today? *(Like friendly small talk.)*

THESPIS: Nothing much. *(He turns a page.)* You?

US: Nothing. Want some? *(We offer the poisoned drink.)*

THESPIS: *(Thespis looks at it for a moment and then turns back to his paper.)* No thanks. *(We are still holding out the drink.)*

US: Thespis? *(We say this like he really needs something to drink on such a hot day. We are concerned for his health and want to let him know he's being stubborn.)*

THESPIS: Yes? *(He does not turn toward us.)*

US: Nothing. *(We withdraw the cup, defeated.)*

Thespis leaps up. "A completely different scene, yes?" We agree. "And yet we didn't change one word, correct?" That is absolutely right, we say. What we did was to change the circumstances. "Correct!" shouts Thespis triumphantly. Acting clearly delights him.

"The playwright only gives us some of the moments of the character's life. It is up to us to create the moments that are implied. In a sense, you see, Stanislavski asks the actor to be a novelist. To fill in all those past, present and even future times that the playwright doesn't have time to show. They must still be part of the inner makeup of the characters we portray, however."

"You did this when you played the scene with me. You filled in some background. You decided that you were coming from school and that I was an abusive father. Those circumstances helped you to act the present moments with me truthfully. If, however, you create circumstances that don't help, but rather hinder your ability to play a scene truthfully, then they are useless."

"If a scene is not working, try deepening the circumstances, or changing them. You see, we do not have names for all the emotions we experience. What, for instance, is the name of the anger we feel when our alarm clock goes off too early? We have none. We just say we are angry about it, or frustrated. But these are global pronouncements without any shading to them. But if we speak of feelings within a well defined circumstance, then we understand the shade of anger we are dealing with. We are not just 'angry,' but we are the kind of 'angry' that happens when our alarm clock goes off too early. And even that is too general."

"More circumstances are needed. Let's say we have been getting good rest for many nights, and that the alarm is only fifteen minutes early. Our anger is likely to be a specific kind of irritation, and not a murderous rage. But if we haven't been sleeping well for days because this alarm has been ringing every three hours, we might pounce on it with tremendous violence. Altering the circumstances, painting them ever more specifically, helps us to find the shadings of emotion for which we have no words."

We think about this. Heaven knows, director's have asked us many times to be MORE angry or MORE upset or LESS agitated. But when we try, we usually fail, and the director becomes MORE and MORE frustrated with us. This is because we do not have the words for the thousand subtle emotions that pass through us each day. We simply do not have a rich enough emotional vocabulary to communicate nuance to each other. Why is this so? Maybe it says something about our society's fear of emotional expression. In any case, if directors painted better circumstances, used more colorful metaphors and imagery, we might understand more specifically what was required of us.

"Yes, you are right," says Thespis. "But if they do not do this, then you must create circumstances which allow you to be MORE angry or MORE upset or LESS agitated and not simply try to squeeze more anger, or more upset, or less agitation out of yourself. Concentrate on what you have to do in the circumstances, not on what you're supposed to feel."

"Now, the playwright only furnishes us with some of the circumstances we need. These we call the givens. Shakespeare tells us that Hamlet is the Prince of Denmark. That's a given. But he tells us nothing about Hamlet's approach to, or arrival at, the castle. That is an imaginary circumstance that we create. We cannot change the given circumstances but we can change and experiment with the imaginary ones. In fact, the imaginary circumstances we create, help us to enter the given ones with a sense of believability."

We're getting a headache. "Relaxation." "Mind, will and emotion." "Concentration." "Public Solitude." "Sensory recall." "Imagination." "Magic If." "Circumstances." Our head is a jumble of phrases and ideas.

"It is a lot, isn't it?" We nod in agreement. "Let's have lunch," Thespis suggests. On a table appears a lucious basket of fruit, a pitcher of water and a loaf of delicious smelling sourdough bread. Butter and jam, of course. We realize that we're famished and sit. As we eat, Thespis speaks gently.

"Relaxation, you see, helps emotion to flow unrestrained. Public Solitude and sensory recall result from concentration, which is a process of our minds. The magic 'if' allows us to enter the circumstances of the character and the play by way of our imaginations. These elements are not separate, although we speak of them that way. They are interrelated, connected to each other. Our imagination is a function of our minds, and yet it also stimulates our feelings. In a given moment, we might focus on one more than another, but they all must work together."

Between bites and gulps, we realize that the will has not been spoken of yet.

"Maybe not spoken of," says Thespis, again picking our thoughts out of the air, "but engaged nonetheless. After I sketched the circumstances of Hamlet's ride, you felt stirred up, didn't you?" We acknowledge that we did. "The circumstances and images stirred feelings in you, yes?" Yes, we reply, they did. "Your body wanted to move, you wanted to do something." Thespis springs up from the table and grabs one of the flags. He holds it up for us to read. It says, ACTION.

But just as we are about to protest the presentation of yet another banner, we smell something. It smells like fire. Our head swivels about, trying to find the source. Our eyes flit to Thespis, who is looking quickly around as well. Maybe it's just one of those old room radiators starting up. But no, there's smoke coming up from under the studio door. Immediately we whip off our jacket and run to the door, while at the same time we search the room with our eyes for a way out. A window, a door, anything. At the door, we bend down and stuff the jacket into the gap between the bottom of it and the floor. We turn back to Thespis. His back is to us. He too is searching for a way out. "No doors, no windows," he says. For a moment no one moves or speaks.

"Through the mirror!" we say, and jump up. "What about the others?" asks Thespis. "We've got to help them." We stop, halfway through the mirror. We look over at the door. A dense smoke is seeping into the room. Thespis's eyes are wild, and we see that he is about to panic. "We'll go through the mirror," we say in a calm voice, "and come out another mirror in this same building. That way we can warn or help the others." Thespis doesn't move. We put out our hand. "Come on. The sooner we're out of here, the sooner we'll be able to help the others."

He stands stock still. "Let's go," we plead. Still, Thespis stands frozen. "THESPIS," we scream, "WE'VE GOT TO LEAVE THIS ROOM!" We grab his arm, but he resists. We wonder if we're going to have to hit him and drag him through the mirror, when he looks right into our eyes. He looks unusually calm. "It's all right," he says with a smile. We think that maybe he has crossed over into some kind of psychotic adjustment to the danger, and for the first time, we are scared.

"Look," he says. Our eyes travel to the door and see that the smoke has stopped. We do not understand. "I did it," Thespis says. Slowly it hits us. Magic. The fire was a trick. We swear at Thespis.

"Forgive me," he says in a soft voice. "I thought you needed to get out of the talking mode. A break, so to speak. From all the talk. Sorry." Can you kill a man who died twenty-five hundred years ago? we wonder. "Please, continue your meal," he says. We slowly sit down, and sip some water. Thespis fetches our jacket and places it in our lap. We are trying to recover from the flood of adrenaline that has been activated. And while Thespis speaks, we curse him.

"ACTION you see. You sprang into action. The circumstances were such that you were impelled to ACT. You see, in a very real sense, you were acting. To be art, you would have to create the smoke, the circumstances and the feelings through your imagination. And the creation of these things would lead you to do something; to act. If you are ever on stage and are doing nothing, then something is terribly wrong. And if you are ever on stage doing something but have no reason for doing it, then something also is terribly wrong. For Stanislavski, acting is doing; doing with a purpose."

"When you went to the door were you worried about how to hold your hands? Or what emotions to feel? Or what expressions your face was making? Of course not. Even as you sit there now, you have an inner action. You are cursing me. You body may be still, but you are full of activity. Quite malicious activity too," he adds under his breath. We feel a little embarrassed. But not too much.

"The point is, that by having an action, you lost any self-conscious awareness of your self. You knew what to do and you did it without worrying about who was watching, or what you looked like." But, we protest that we weren't acting. We really thought the building was on fire. We were only doing what we would do in life.

"True," replies Thespis. "So let's act." Oh no, there goes our adrenaline again.

"Imagine this part of the room as the hallway to your apartment. Imagine that you are coming home from work at the end of the day, and that all you want to do is drop into your comfortable chair and put your feet up. This is the thought in your mind as you approach the imaginary door. But when you get halfway down the hallway, you smell smoke. Go ahead, try it."

We stand up and begin walking toward the door. The thought of dropping into a nice overstuffed chair right now has great appeal. We can even "see" its green color and almost feel its plush texture. But a moment later our thoughts are interrupted by an awareness. We take a few more steps, then stop. We look around and sniff the air, puzzled. Smells like smoke. Our eyes scan the hallway until we realize that the white billows we see are coming from under the door of our apartment. We run to it.

"Your wife and daughter are inside," says Thespis.

Immediately, we put our hand on the door to open it. But it is too hot to touch. We freeze for a moment. We have to do something to get them out. We kick at the imaginary door.

"It does not give," says Thespis in a quiet voice.

We kick it harder.

"Still it does not give."

We don't know that to do. We are breathing hard. "Help!" we scream. "Fire!"

"There is no one else in the building," says Thespis.

We are getting desperate. We look around for some means of help. In the hallway of our own apartment, in real life, is a fire extinguisher box with an axe inside. We decide that this hallway too, has one. We run to the imaginary box, thrust our fist through it, and take out the axe. As we rush back to the door, we see that our hand is bleeding. No matter, we've got to get through that door to our wife and daughter. We swing the imaginary axe at the door over and over until it gives way. Immediately, we have to cover our eyes and turn our heads away from the escaping smoke. The rush of heat pushes us back. They must be dead we think as we run back for the fire extinguisher. We've got to hurry. Maybe they're alive. In the doorway, we unleash the extinguishing spray and slowly advance into the room. Where are they? We try to see through the smoke but it is too thick. We call out.

"Debby? Jenny? Where are you? Debby? Jenny? I'm here by the door. Where are you? Answer me, if you can. Where are you?"

We have been moving all through the space. Suddenly we trip over the body of our daughter.

"Oh my God." We put the fire extinguisher down and pick up her limp body. Without stopping to listen for a heartbeat or to check for a breath, we rush her out of the room.

"Good," says Thespis. "You may stop. The scene is over."

We stand breathless, still holding our arms out. We look over at Thespis.

"You can drop your arms now," Thespis reminds us.

"Is she dead or alive?" we ask.

"Don't know yet," he replies. "Good time for an act break though, don't you think?"

We laugh. We are grateful for a little humor after this harrowing experience. We drop our arms and head for the water.

"This time, you were acting, yes?"

"Yes," we reply.

"You are a good actor," Thespis says. "You have a strong *sense of truth.* None of this actually happened, but you believed so strongly in the circumstance that you acted as if your apartment was on fire."

"Did you have feelings while you were engaged in this scene?" Of course, we reply. "Were you aware of the different expressions on your face, or what postures your body took? Did you think about Aaron Hill? About which face to make that would communicate the proper emotion to your audience? Did you think about Delsarte, and which body position would best represent the feelings you were having?" Not really, we respond. "Were you acting this time? Did you act truthfully the imaginary circumstances you were given?" Yes, we say, this time we really were acting. You had a strong action to play didn't you?" Yes, we reply. "What was it?" he asks. Uh oh, a test. It was to get the door open, we answer. "That was certainly an important action," he agrees. "Were there other actions involved? Did you have to do things in order to get the door open?" Of course, we say. We had to try to turn the door handle, we had to try kicking the door, we had to smash the glass containing the axe and the fire extinguisher, we had to get the axe and we had to swing the axe until the door gave way.

"Good," say Thespis. "Lots of little actions were necessary to accomplish the larger action. And each little action helped you toward your goal of getting the door open. The situation compelled your body to react, and you did. The circumstance led to feeling which led to action. Or did it?"

"So much ink has been spilled over whether actors should work from the external to the internal, from the outside to the inside, or from the internal to the external, that it has gotten a bit ridiculous. In this exercise there was a clear connection between your inner self and your body, was there not?" We agree that there was. Our inner understanding of the situation caused our body to go into action. "Or did running toward the door cause your inner feelings?" Thespis asks. Truthfully, we cannot really separate this out.

"You see, arousing feeling is something like trying to understand the nature of light. Is light a wave, or a particle? This question puzzled physicists of your century for many years. They felt that it had to be one or the other. But finally they had to accept a strange fact. They had to accept the paradox that sometimes light acts like a wave and sometimes light acts like a particle. Light, it turns out, is not so simple. Doesn't want to be pinned down. The same is true in arousing emotion. It is a paradox. Sometimes emotion comes from inside and results in some action. But sometimes, action itself causes us to feel emotion. Remember Delsarte's soldier? How, when he was posed in a position of fear, he became fearful?"

"If you make a fist, for example, and begin pounding the table, you will soon begin to feel anger. An anger stimulated only by the action of banging and not by some circumstance that angered you." We think we're getting the point. Thespis seems to be proposing some kind of quantum theory of emotion. This ancient Greek certainly keeps up. "The mind-body connection is one that Stanislavski is acutely aware of. He knows that 'All external production is formal, cold, and pointless if it is not motivated from within.'18 But we're not ready for that yet."

Thespis comes over to the table and sits. He eats some grapes.

"You did very well in that scene. Of course, it was only one brief exercise, and there was very little dialogue." He pops a grape into his mouth. "Imagine the work involved in determining the actions of an entire play. All of the outer and inner actions. It would be a lot to keep in one's mind and still feel spontaneous, don't you think?" We do. "Yet it must be done. As preparation, you see." Our heart sinks a little. "But there is a way to do it all quite simply. At least according to Stanislavski."

"When you smelled the imaginary smoke in the scene you just did, what did you wish?" We think for a moment. "It's really pretty simple," says Thespis. "And if you use an active verb in your statement, then what you wish will be related to an action, since a verb is an action word." Now we are confused. "Well," coaxes Thespis, "did you wish to save your family, perhaps?" Yes, we reply, yes we did.

"That wish is what Stanislavski calls an OBJECTIVE. It's an unfortunate term in that it is so...well...objective. It sounds so dispassionate and neutral. But that would be the opposite of Stanislavski's intention. It is much better to think of the 'object' in the word 'objective' as the object of your desire. So, in the case of your scene, the object of your desire was to save your wife and child. Correct?" Yes, we reply, that's right.

"Could you phrase it in a more active way, with an image that would attract you?" We're not quite sure what he means. We need help with this, we say.

"Well," begins Thespis, "after you smell that smoke, could the object of your desire be to snatch your loved ones from the fires of hell? To win the race with the flames? To beat death? Don't these ways of phrasing your objective quicken your blood and make you strain to fulfill them? Don't they engage your imagination and body more than the phrase 'save my family'? The great danger of an objective is that it can easily become just an intellectual construct. Dry as dust. That does not help us as actors."

"Perhaps now you also see that your actions were in support of your objective. Trying to open the door was one way to get inside and snatch your family from the flames of death. But it didn't work. You began to fall behind in your race. That impelled you to another action; kicking the door. But that also didn't work. Desperation built, as time became your greatest enemy. You ran down the hall and cut your hand getting an axe. Another action in support of your objective. Each action was natural and logical, given your objective. You didn't do anything that contradicted that objective.

Now, of course, you didn't think about it in this way. You simply responded to the given circumstances with all your heart. But if the circumstances did not engage you instincts, working on actions and objectives could create fertile enough ground to attract your true intuitive responses. Remember, if acting is to be alive, your mind, your will and your emotions must be engaged. The objective activates your will to action. Emotion will follow, as you pursue the 'object of your desire.' Do you see?"

We admit that we are beginning to.

We confess to Thespis that the word "objective" has terrified us from the time we first heard it. But that now, the way he's talking about it, it seems less abstract and more exciting.

"Good. This talk of objectives can be quite tricky. In any case, when you are working on a part, you work out the objectives and the actions that support them. Not in a dry way, but in an imaginative and passionate one. Doing this, gives the actor a pathway through a script; markers that help him know which way to go. By breaking a play down into objectives and actions, the actor has no time for self-consciousness and cannot focus on forcing emotions through his body. As Stanislavski says, '…don't worry about the flower, just water the roots…'"[19]

"And yet keeping in mind each separate action and objective would simply be too much for an actor to do while performing. So Stanislavkski suggests that the actor keep his eye on this." Thespis turns over a banner that reads SUPER-OBJECTIVE.

"In a play, the super-objective is like the theme. In *Hamlet,* the super-objective might be stated as, the taking of revenge leads only to tragedy."

"All of the actions of the play, indeed of each character, should point towards and shed light on this main idea. If the main idea were stated in a different way, then the actions illuminating that idea would be different. Before going onstage, the actor can remind herself of the super-objective, and since all the smaller actions and objectives are contained in it, she will quickly be pointed in the right direction. She doesn't need to remind herself of each action and objective through the whole play. This would simply serve to distract her from living spontaneously on the stage."

"Think of objectives as magnets that pull you through a performance. The super-objective is the main magnet to which all the others adhere. Stanislavski's idea here reminds me of what Plato said about inspiration, "This stone (the magnet) not only attracts iron rings, but also imparts to them a similar power of attracting other rings; and sometimes you may see a number of pieces of iron and rings suspended from one another so as to form quite a long chain; and all of them derive their power of suspension from the original stone."[20]

"You see, all of the smaller objectives are like a chain of magnets connected to the largest and strongest one which is the super-objective." A chain of magnets. Pulling us through the play. We like that.

"And like the smaller objectives which give rise to actions, the super-objective gives rise to the THROUGH LINE OF ACTION. This simply means that all of the actions of your character create a clear line leading to the fulfillment of the super-objective."

We confess to Thespis that our head is swimming.

"Let me try to be clear. Simply put, the objective is what you want, and the action is what you do. Together they involve the total actor, his inner life and its outward expression. Have a peach."

We do. "You see, you want relief," says Thespis, "that's your objective. So, you eat a peach, that's your action. Simple. It's the words that get in the way."

"I think we need a little perspective here," says Thespis. "All of this work does not make you a good actor, or even guarantee a good performance. Pursuing an objective is not acting." We groan. What then is the point of doing all this, we wonder.

"This system, created by Stanislavski, is meant to prepare the ground for that ever elusive gift, inspiration. Doing this work is like erecting lightning rods to attract lightning. The more rods you build and the better you build them, the more likely the bolt will strike. Really, this system itself is a magnet for the subconscious. Because for Stanislavski, the subconscious is the source of inspiration."

"The promise of his system is this; if you use your imagination to enter, with belief, the imaginary circumstances of the play, and if you follow the correct objectives and actions through the play's length, then the proper emotions will follow you and inspiration will more likely come."

That sounds a little more manageable to us, we admit. Maybe the peach is helping. But something is bothering us. What happens, we ask, if the emotion doesn't come? We are thinking of a time when we were supposed to cry on stage and just couldn't do it.

"Good question, says Thespis. "Stanislavski has an answer for this, but it is the most controversial aspect of his work." Thespis picks up a flag that reads, EMOTION MEMORY.

"In the year 1900, a book called *The Psychology of the Emotions,* by the French psychologist Théodule Ribot, was translated into Russian. Stanislavski read it and was greatly influenced by it. Ribot stated that the memory of all of life's experiences are recorded in the nervous system.[21] To Stanislavski this meant that the actor should be able to call up emotions from his past and apply them to the emotional life of the character. To activate these remembered emotions is the tricky part. Stanislavski used the idea of *sense memory* as the trigger."

"If the feelings of some past event in your life do not immediately come to you," Thespis went on, "you then concentrate on what you saw and heard, on what you did and where you were. Recalling those sensory details will bring back the feelings associated with them. The trick is to focus on the physical memories and let the emotions come. If your character is called upon to cry at a certain moment in the play, and you as the actor cannot produce the required tears, you can use emotion memory to arouse the proper feeling. Remember a time when you cried. But do not focus on the feeling. focus instead on where you were standing, what you did, what you saw and what you heard. If you were standing by a drinking fountain when the news of your father's death really hit you, see yourself at that fountain, see its color, see your hand on the handle, hear the flow of the water, feel the slowness of time, see where your mother is, remember your brother saying 'it's up to us now,' and let the emotions come. You can then use your own personal feelings in the role to bring it alive."

"For Stanislavski, the remembered feeling does not have to be one that the actor has experienced directly. It might be a feeling generated by seeing something happen to someone else, or through reading. If feelings are stimulated by these things, the actor can still use them. The real point is that these remembered emotions are controllable and repeatable. Emotion memories are not useful if they cannot be controlled or repeated."

"But using recalled emotion is only one of *several* ways to arouse emotion. Sometimes a strong objective will stimulate feeling, sometimes a powerful circumstance will start emotions flowing, sometimes a vivid image will arouse sleeping emotions, sometimes an action will bring a feeling alive, sometimes an object of attention will animate your emotional life, and often, your interaction with the other actors will stimulate your feelings."

"There are many paths to your feelings without forcing them. Feelings are notoriously elusive and if you reach for them directly, they will run from you. Even in emotion memory, we do not focus on emotion itself. We focus on everything around it."

We remind Thespis that he said emotion memory is the most controversial aspect of Stanislavski's work. What, we wonder, is the controversy about?

"I won't tell you," he announces. "Not now. Later, you will understand. I will only tell you that Stanislavski himself stopped using it toward the end of his life. But that doesn't mean that you should disregard it. He always felt that you must bring your emotional life to the parts you play. But they must always be at the service of the play and the character, and not mere personal indulgence."

Thespis turns over another banner. This one says COMMUNION. "A moment ago, I spoke of the other actors, and their affect on you. This is a crucial part of Stanislasvki's system. The living exchange between the characters in a scene, the communion between them, is what rivets the audiences attention. The completeness of that communion helps each individual in the auditorium forget himself, and enter into the drama on stage. This is another kind of communion; the audience with the characters, with the story."

Thespis has been standing for quite a long time, and he looks tired. We think he might need a rest.

"I am talking to you now, and you are attentive to me. My words have meaning to you. But if my breathing were to become irregular while I spoke, and the color were to drain from my face, you would become concerned..."

We are becoming concerned.

"...and you would be listening to me in a somewhat different way. You would be responding less to what I was saying, and more to the way I was saying it. The essence of the scene would shift from understanding the information of my words, to a concern for my health and safety. You would be responding to messages from my body, you would be sensing my internal distress..."

He looks very pale.

"...you would be listening to what is going on beneath the words, to what Stanislavski called the subtext. Often, the actual words of a scene are like the tips of icebergs. They are what we see, but most of their meaning is below them. They are surface manifestations of deep inner workings..."

We are sitting on the edge of our seat.

"... like sunspots...which appear on the surface of the sun, but...are the result of violent...storms...deeper down..."

Thespis falls to one knee, and we rush to him. His breathing is labored and his body is hot. We help him to a chair and put a cup of water to his lips. He drinks.

"Thank you," he says. His voice is low and congested. He takes another drink. "All of this...traveling, I think." Yes, we agree. He must be quite worn down by all this jumping around through time and space.

"I cannot do this much longer, I'm afraid. Fetch my cothorni, would you?" He indicates his thick-soled footwear. We get them. "You see," he slowly continues, "had I said those words about subtext in my normal healthy way...you would have reacted differently. But beneath my words was a circumstance, a situation that changed the way I...said them and the way you reacted to them. You became sensitive to more than my words and reacted accordingly. You were playing me and not just what I was...saying. This is so crucial. This relationship between the characters is really what the audience came to see. The living chemistry between us is what is compelling. When actors have an affect on each other; when one action causes a reaction in the other character which causes a reaction in the first character then the most precious exchange in the theater is taking place.."

"I don't have much time left before I must go, so I must finish. Stanislavski's ideas are basic to your understanding of what lies ahead. He worked so hard to help actors have a practical way to approach acting. But you must always remember that his quest never ended. He always looked for new and better ways to train actors. He regarded them as artists and what they did as a high art. No matter what path you follow, keep alive your respect for both the search and the searcher. He did."

"Now, in a scene, suppose that your action does not lead to the successful fulfillment of your objective. Do you...give up? Not likely. You try a new way to get it. Sometimes a scene requires that you try many new actions to get what you want. This shifting of actions in response to new circumstances is what Stanislavski called, ADAPTATION."

"If I wanted to borrow money from you, I might begin with some small talk to disarm your defenses. I might use the adaptation of charm to make you feel good about talking to me. Then I might tell you, with obvious embarrassment, about my grave financial situation, hoping to gain your sympathy. Then, I might adopt a tone of directness, look you straight in the eye, and ask you for a loan. If you refuse, I must adapt to that reality, that circumstance. My adaptation might be to plead with you or to use guilt as a means of getting what I want. You see, the objective of getting the money never changed, only the adaptations I had to make in order to get it, changed."

"The use of many adaptations in a scene lends it color and variety. If you use only a single means of securing what you want in a scene (and some scenes do require this), it usually becomes boring. Review for yourself, the adaptations you made both to me and to the circumstances when we played the scene with the poisoned drink. I haven't time to do it with you now."

"Turn over that one." Thespis points to a flag on the floor and we pick it up. It reads, TEMPO-RHYTHM. "Yes," smiles Thespis, "one of my favorites."

"Tempo is the speed, of course. Rhythm is the accent. A fast waltz is usually accented, ONE-two-three, ONE-two-three. A march is usually accented ONE-two-three-four, ONE-two-three-four."

We wonder what this has to do with realistic and truthful acting. Sounds like some mechanical approach, not like Stanislavski at all.

"Not like Stanislavski? Where do you get such ideas? Do you know he trained actors to move to a metronome? Do you know he spent much time schooling actors in voice, diction and movement? Are you aware of the fact that he was concerned that actors develop a sense of proportion?"

Meaning what, we ask.

"Meaning that all objectives, all actions are not created equal. Some are more important than others. If you put too much emphasis on a minor objective or action, you hurt the overall structure of your part. How many times have I seen an actor or a student give every object of attention, every action and every objective the same weight. Sometimes, you put down a cup of water while talking and it's not a matter of life and death." He puts down the cup. "As a Mr. Sigmund Freud said in your century, 'sometimes a cigar is just a cigar.'"

"It takes time to learn all this, of course, and so Stanislavski allowed two years of training in order for the actor to get all the parts of his system in place. The first year he called, 'work on the self' and the second year he called, 'work on the role.' But back to tempo-rhythm."

"Have you ever noticed the profound effect an inner tempo-rhythm has on you? When, for example, you were watching me weaken just a few moments ago, what was your inner tempo?" We say that it was very fast. "Just so," comments Thespis. "What was the tempo-rhythm of my speech?" Slow and halting, we say. "Quite," is the reply.

"The power of tempo-rhythm can best be demonstrated from the outside. Start walking at a slow measured pace. As the left foot comes forward, bring the right one up to it. Pause for a slight moment and then step forward on the right foot, bringing the left even with it." We try this. After a few steps we suddenly feel that we are walking down the aisle at a wedding. We imagine, without any effort at all, people standing on either side of us. We don't feel like the groom, but more like a child walking ahead of the wedding couple and we feel both embarrassed and excited.

"You see," says Thespis, "the tempo-rhythm and manner of your walk suggested not only a circumstance, but aroused feelings as well. It is a truly powerful thing. If you like, it is working from the outside to the inside. And yes, Stanislavski used this method extensively, both as an actor and as a director. There is more to this man than you may, at first, have thought."

"Suppose, you must disarm a bomb. Inside, your tempo-rhythm would probably be wild, your heart beating furiously. But outside, sudden movements brought on by your inner anxiety might set the bomb off. You would have to move slowly and precisely. This battle between inner and outer tempo-rhythms can create tremendous tension on the stage. Look to it."

"Let me summarize." Thespis has put on his cothorni, and his mask. Slowly, he stands. His voice is suddenly very powerful. "For Stanislavski there is both an inner and an outer technique that the actor must acquire. The inner technique consists of *imagination, concentration, magic 'if,' given circumstances, sense of truth, public solitude, sensory recall, objectives, actions, emotion memory, inner tempo-rhythms.* The outer technique, which is intimately connected to the inner, consists of *relaxation, voice, diction, movement, acrobatics, outer tempo-rhythm.*"[22]

"This system never remained static. It was evolving even at Stanislavski's death in 1938. You will learn later what he ultimately came to believe about the use of emotion memory. But it is important now to understand his *method of psycho-physical actions.* He came to believe that working on a part was best done when the actors laid out the physical actions early on in rehearsal. After a thorough absorption of the circumstances of the play, the actors would enact the physical actions, improvising the dialogue as they went along. In this way, the words would not blind the actors from seeing the actions and objectives underlying each scene. As they rehearsed, the circumstances and actions would deepen until finally, the author's words were put to use. This method is based on a profound belief that 'movement and thought are inseparable.'[23] Unfortunately, Stanislavski died before he could fully explore or articulate this method, and it remains for many, the most tantalizing part of his work."

"This whole system of Stanislavski's is the most complete and practical yet devised for the training of an actor. It is designed to create that receptive shore over which the waves of inspiration can flow."

"It does not promise, however, to make you a great actor. According to Stanislavski, acting cannot be taught. His method is simply a means, not an end. It is meant to keep falseness and cliché out of the theater. It is meant to transport the audience into the reality of the imagination; to take them out of the theater and into the world of the characters. With the result that a mutual and beautiful communal act of the imagination takes place between the author, the actors and the spectators."

"Many have added to Stanislavski's system, and many have criticized and rejected it. But it remains the baseline, the beginning point, of all serious discussions about this elusive craft."

"He created a true ensemble of artists wherein even the smallest parts were crafted by loving actors, and brought to life with the same care and attention lavished on the leading roles. He created an ensemble not of supporting and star actors, but an ensemble of dedicated professionals, each capable of the highest level of work."

"This man, who struggled through so much failure, achieved an astonishing success. His productions ended when the final curtains rang down, but his quest, his passion and his discoveries remain an everlasting legacy. He found nuggets of the purest gold, and shared them with the world."

"But you have much to explore. Much to learn. And I must journey homeward." As he steps through the mirror, we hear the simple word, "Good-bye."

Chapter 3

Smashing the Fourth Wall

By the time the Moscow Art Theater toured the United States in early 1923, it was world renowned. But at home, in Russia, it had been under attack for some years. The first challenges came from the MAT's "special" playwright, Anton Chekhov himself.

Chekhov objected to the surface detail that Stanislavski brought to the production of his plays. He made a joke in front of Stanislavski about the director's use of the sounds of every day life in his productions, "I'm going to write a new play, which will begin like this 'How nice it is! How quiet! Not a bird to be heard, not a clock, not a bell, not a single cricket...'"[1] But Chekhov's objections went much deeper. He felt that Stanislavski did not understand his plays and missed the comic element in them. He did not like Stanislavski's interpretation of his characters, and felt that his work was misrepresented. And yet, he knew that the artistic finish of the MAT's productions were superior to all others, and continued to let Danchenko and Stanislavsky produce his plays.

Other challenges came from three young members of the Moscow Art Theater itself.

In 1911, a young actor, twenty years Stanislavski's junior, joined the MAT. One year later this remarkable man, Evgeni Vakhtangov, was a co-founder of the Moscow Art Theater's First Studio. There, he began directing and teaching actors.

His first productions were marked by such extreme emotional realism, that Stanislavski felt the acting had crossed over into hysteria. By 1915, Vakhtangov's experiments at the First Studio began to yield fruit, bringing a new discipline to his acting and directing, and by 1918 he was beginning to explore some new ideas that went beyond his mentor.

Vakhtangov wanted to combine Stanislavski's inner technique with a vivid and exciting theatricalism. The theater, he felt, was not like life, but a place that required its own special form of expression. It should be pointed out again, that Stanislavski also did not believe that the theater was the same thing as everyday life. He strongly objected to this way of thinking. He also did not feel that the actor should "live" the part so much as "experience" the part.[2]

But Vakhtangov was interested in exploring what he called the "grotesque." For him, "Grotesque is a method which enables the actor and the director to justify inwardly the vivid, condensed content of a given play."[3] By approaching a play through the grotesque aesthetic, the actors could exaggerate and distort the characters. But in order to do this successfully, they had to base their characterizations on inner truth. In this way, Vakhtangov extended the Stanislavski system to include a kind of "fantastic realism." A realism which encompassed theatricality.

Vakhtangov felt that "Stanislavsky demanded...that the audience forget that it is in the theater, that it came to feel itself living in the atmosphere and milieu in which the characters of the play live...Stanislavsky wanted to destroy theatrical banality...but (he) also removed a certain genuine, necessary theatricality, and genuine theatricality consists in presenting theatrical works in a theatrical manner."[4] Notice here, that while Stanislavski wanted the audience to forget it was in a theater, that it was watching the play through an imaginary fourth wall, he never wanted the actor to forget that there was an audience present.

Stanislavski was so impressed with the achievements of Vakhtangov and his actors, that he appointed Vakhtangov director of the MAT's First Studio.

One of the new ideas that Vakhtangov brought to the system was his notion of "adjustment" or "justification." This radical idea suggested that an actor could use motivations, play actions completely unrelated to the content of the play. "A performer who is directed to pace the stage and think of avenging his father's death...may not be stimulated by the director's suggestion and find no inner reality in the action. But he could pretend to himself that the purpose of his pacing is to find a weak floorboard in order to fall through the stage and sue the theater's management!"[5] No one would know, not the audience, not the director, not even his fellow players, that the actor is playing this circumstance. It can be his secret. Instead of looking to the character's past to justify the actions of the present, the actor can use immediate and unrelated circumstances to justify his behavior. Be bold. Try it.

Suppose you have a scene wherein you're meant to act and speak out of a righteous anger you simply do not feel. You might find the feeling you need by playing a secret unrelated to the events of the play. Be angry at the director who has not helped you enough and now strands you on stage with a ruined performance. How dare he do that to you, to any actor? Now try the actions and words of the scene. It will crackle. And the director need never know. There is something delicious in this. Savor it.

But Vakhtangov went further than this. He felt that each actor needed a reason to even come to the theater and to get on the stage. For example, you might feel that every character ever written exists as a ghost hovering in the spaces above the stage. You might believe that each one desperately longs to have it's story told, but is incapable of doing so without help. You might feel that every character has this right to have it's story told, to have it's day in court, and that you are the one hope your particular character has to live again for a few brief hours. Whether a good character or an evil one, you feel the responsibility, the duty, the honor to give passionate form to this disembodied ghost. And for this reason, you will step from the wings into the playing space. Such an overall justification allows the actor to put herself in the service of something larger. It creates a unique bond between the actor and the character that transcends the merely personal. It gives the actor a reason for doing what she does beyond simple ego-gratification. It makes the actor's work, holy.

An exercise Vakhtangov would use with his students involved striking a pose and then finding a justification for it. For example, lift your arms high over your head, and stretch up as high as you can. Hold this position and then create a reason for it. Fill the pose with the inner action that you are reaching for something on a top shelf, or that you are on a cliff and are reaching for a rescuer's rope, or that you are poised on an Olympic diving board, or that you are being arrested. In this way, the physical can come first and then be given an inner life.

Stanislavski called Vakhtangov the greatest teacher of his system. His work and ideas had a profound effect on the Americans who later formed the Group Theater. Lee Strasberg, one of those founders, felt that, "Vakhtangov's value lay in dissociating the Stanislavski System as a technique for the actor, from the Stanislavski method of production…the 'Method' in the proper hands did not produce only realistic acting, but that the process of 'inner justification' was a necessary technique in a creative process regardless of the style desired."[6]

It would be wise to remember, however, that pigeonholing Stanislavski as hostile to theatricalism is a frustrating pastime. Vakhtangov was shocked for example when, in 1917, Stanislavski took over a production of *Twelfth Night* from another director, and had action spilling out into the auditorium, actors running down the aisles and appearing from behind the audience. "It was an overt display of 'theatricality.'"[7] Stanislavski was no ideologue. He was a practical man of the theater, and if a play called for a measure of theatricality, he used it.

Vakhtangov's theater was a true celebration of the imagination. He was not bound by any unnecessary fidelity to surface realism. He reached into the center of a work and exploded it on to the stage.

What this astonishing man might have achieved, had he lived longer, simply boggles the mind. But sick with cancer, he died in the spring of 1922 at the age of thirty-nine. "The news of his death reached the Moscow theaters at once, and all audiences rose in tribute."[8]

❄

Admitted to the Moscow Art Theater in 1912 was another man destined to extend Stanislavski's system. He was Michael Chekhov, a nephew of the playwright Anton Chekhov. His performances in the early twenties, in plays like Gogol's *Inspector General* and Strindberg's *Erik XIV,* stamped him as a genius. He displayed a unique ability to remain believable on stage while behaving in the most eccentric manner.

Chekhov's use of Vakhtangov's "justification" was so imaginative that those around him were startled by his inventiveness. When playing a drunk, he avoided the usual clichés and "built the physical character on a madman's realization that each part of his body is dying in a separate and horrible way."[9] He felt that Stanislavski slighted the imagination in his system, and he was determined to return it to a place of primary importance.

He rejected the idea that an actor was restricted to emotional memories from his own life and did not see why the actor could not use imaginary events and images to stimulate feelings. He felt that using one's own experiences exclusively would soon exhaust the actor's emotional resources, and that after a while, actor's would begin imitating themselves. Stanislavski's response to this was that the actor must always be closely observing others so that an inexhaustible source of emotional life was always available.

For Chekhov, this was not enough. Why not give the imagination the importance it deserves? Why can't an actor search for emotional stimulation from things that have never happened to anyone, or are impossible, but suggestive? Why not imagine walking on the surface of the moon with it's one-sixth less gravitational pull? Wouldn't a feeling of giddiness and joy result? Why must the actor go into his personal past in order to stimulate such a feeling?

Chekhov began to talk of "atmospheres" and "qualities" in his teaching and looked for the little moments, which he referred to as "jewelry," that gave performances a shining indelibility. He felt that "atmospheres" could lead actors to emotional responses more reliably than emotion memory could.

So what are these "atmospheres" and "qualities"? According to Chekhov, atmospheres are "the source of ineffable moods and waves of feeling that emanate from one's surroundings."[10] We have all felt the effect of walking into a room and being swept by a feeling of fear or of well-being. Chekhov wanted his actors to be sensitive to atmosphere because of its influence on behavior and emotion. An exercise in atmosphere might involve having an actor imagine that he is being followed down a foggy street. The atmosphere of tension and fear would naturally follow without the actor having to work hard to create it. Chekhov's idea here is to combine a circumstance with a sense memory. The fusion of these two elements elicits an immediate emotional response that is playable by the actor.

If one extends this, one realizes that every play, every scene, is permeated with atmospheres. They can be physical, such as a sweltering hot day, or psychological, like a feeling of foreboding. Living within an atmosphere gives an overall direction to the way an actor pursues her objective or executes an action. If our action is to bend down and tie our shoelace, we will do it differently in an atmosphere of impending danger than we will in an atmosphere of safety and calm.

What is the atmosphere in the space you're in right now? Look up from this book and "feel" the room. What does it say to you? What do you say back to it? Imagine a different atmosphere. It can be from a play, from your life, or from your boundless imagination. Get up and walk slowly through it. What feelings does it stir up?

Imagine the atmosphere at the beginning of Anton Chekhov's *The Cherry Orchard:*[11] "Dawn; The sun will soon rise. It is May, the cherry trees are in bloom, but it is cold in the orchard; there is a morning frost. The windows in the room are closed." Go ahead and wander through the orchard at this early morning hour. Not as any particular character at first, just as yourself. Go ahead, I'll wait.

❄

Nice isn't it? Imagine if this cherry orchard was your very own. Now go inside the house. It's warmer because the windows are shut.

Imagine the freedom. You get to be in this house without any of the characters knowing about it. You can look around, even spy on them as they sleep. The better you know the play the more the room will speak to you. Now go back outside to the orchard and wander through again as the light of the day comes up. But wander it now knowing that you must sell it. Knowing that soon, you will not see it again. Now walk through it as though you will be the new owner. Different feelings and thoughts are aroused aren't they?

You begin to see how powerful it would be to walk through the cherry orchard as every different character in the play. The atmosphere of it brings circumstances and feelings along with it. Chekhov's world is a world of the imagination and gives great value to what is today called creative visualization. It is little wonder that he writes about the character Don Quixote with such deep affection. Like that character, Michael Chekhov could use his brilliant and even feverish imagination to transform the commonplace into the magical.

The inventive use of atmospheres can open up new possibilities for the actor and greatly help him to enter into the reality of imaginary circumstances. And yet there is a danger. If an actor only plays the atmosphere of a scene, he runs the risk of playing a mood all the way through it. And "mood" spelled backwards is "doom." If an actor plays a mood through a scene, he is likely to miss the many spontaneous moments, separate actions and emotional shifts that make up the dynamics of that scene. So, be careful.

Visualization also plays an important role in Chekhov's conception of characterization. He asks actors to "see" the character and notice how he is dressed, how he moves, what he does. Further, he encourages the actor to ask questions of the character: "Show me how you run, how you cry, how you sit, how you laugh." In this way the actor arrives at character decisions in a living, vivid way and not just through an exercise of the intellect.

What about "qualities"? Chekhov uses this word as a substitute for emotion. He realizes that asking for a feeling directly is often the best way to make it run and hide. So instead of saying "be more happy here," says "add a quality of happiness to what you are doing."

But his greatest extension of the system came from what he termed the "psychological gesture." Robert Lewis, an original member of the Group Theater, co-founder of the Actor's Studio, and a celebrated director and teacher, describes a vivid example of its use in his book *Method Or Madness.* "Chekhov was playing an American businessman. He had bickered and fought with his partner all through the first act but now, in the second act, he was going to try to make it up…As Chekhov was talking, his hands started to dig into the man's heart. Suddenly one got this terrific image of what love is—the wanting to become one with somebody…He was feeling it all inside to the full, but he had chosen a way to express it which was brilliant."

The psychological gesture is a physical action which reveals the inner feelings and personality of the character. In the late 1970's Michael Moriarty played the title part in Shakespeare's play *Richard The Third,* directed by Mel Shapiro at Lincoln Center in New York City.

From the beginning of the play, Richard's goal is to become the King of England. Finally, his path is viciously cleared of all obstacles and he is ready to ascend the throne.

When the moment of Richard's coronation came, Michael Moriarty was kneeling at the downstage lip of the stage facing the audience. Directly upstage of him sat the vacant throne. Moriarty, still on his knees, turned toward it. And then a startling thing happened.

Instead of rising as expected and walking ceremoniously to it, Moriarty toddled the twenty feet to the throne on his knees. He looked like a three year old. It was startling to see, and at first the audience chuckled. But before he was halfway there, the audience was still. Richard's naked craving for the throne was suddenly clear. It had the single-minded power of a child's desire for the brightest object in a toy store. It was primal. His murderous rampage to the throne was simply an unbridled tantrum. In this grown-up nobleman burned the untamed tyrannical will of a baby, and like a baby, when he got what he wanted, he quickly tired of it.

After the crown was placed on Moriarty's head, he slouched in the throne and didn't seem to know what to do. He'd gotten his bauble, but now didn't know what to do with it. This audacious psychological gesture illuminated more about Richard's inner character than anything else in the play. Moriarty made clear the bond between the adult lust for power and the unreasoning willfulness of a child. Such boldness makes a performance indelible, and illustrates what Chekhov wants the actor to accomplish.

But this example is a bit of an exception. Chekhov does not usually intend for the psychological gesture to be externalized. Rather, he intends for it to be discovered in rehearsal and then internalized during performance. For example, he writes, "Take a certain gesture, such as 'to grasp.' Do it physically...Now on the basis of this gesture, which you will do inwardly, say the sentence, 'Please darling, tell me the truth.' While speaking, produce the gesture inwardly...Now do them together—the gesture and the sentence. Then drop the physical gesture and speak, having the gesture inside only."[12] Doing this inner gesture gives the sentence an intensity and feeling it otherwise would not have, and the source of this power is repeatable because it is based on a repeatable bodily action. If the feeling is lost at some point during a performance, the actor simply recalls the gesture (and could practice the grasping action offstage) in order to rediscover the missing intensity of the line.

Michael Chekhov is one of the few actors from the Moscow Art Theater whom we can easily see today. Rent Alfred Hitchcock's 1945 film, *Spellbound*, and you can see this remarkable man ply his craft. (For other film performances of teachers, see the Video Bibliography at the back of this book.) Chekhov died in Hollywood in 1955 at the age of sixty-four.

Vakhtangov and Chekhov often worked together and influenced each other. They unloosed the imaginative and fantastical element in Stanislavski's system in a way that Stanislavski himself did not. They rescued his work from being applied solely to a realistic acting style. But neither of them broke with the system, they extended and enlarged it. Another figure would go further.

As a young man, Vsevolod Meyerhold was overwhelmed by Stanislavski's portrayal of Othello, and became an original member of the Moscow Art Theater. He spent four years with the MAT and originated the roles of Treplev in *The Seagull,* and Tusenbach in *The Three Sisters.*

But in 1903, he left the company to start a theater of his own. He left not because of any bad feeling toward Stanislavski, but because of problems with Nemirovich-Danchenko. When he returned to Moscow two years later, he was a changed man. His experiments with his own company had taken him in a new direction and they excited him so much that Stanislavski himself became infected with Meyerhold's enthusiasm and set him up in a studio of his own.

But when the work of this new studio was presented, it was a disaster. Stanislavski lost a good deal of money and he was forced to stop the enterprise altogether. Meyerhold was caught between the realism he had practiced at the Moscow Art Theater and his desire to transcend it.

The failure of his first experimental studio compelled Meyerhold to rethink his ideas. He realized that a new type of actor training was needed, that the fatal flaw with Stanislavski's actors was their lack of physical expressivity. In 1907 Meyerhold denounced "...the Art Theater as obsolete, bogged down in naturalism and literal realism."[13] Meyerhold wanted to do away with the idea of a fourth wall, and involve and confront the audience directly. Why should art imitate life when art is so utterly different from life? Why should spectators feel they are peeping through a keyhole like a voyeur when watching an act of theater? The realistic theater of the MAT, Meyerhold felt, only made the middle and upper classes feel comfortable. They were not challenged.

Revolution was in the air. By 1914, Pablo Picasso had changed the view of art, Igor Stravinski had shaken music to its core, Albert

Einstein had overturned Newton's universe, Charles Darwin had altered our view of the natural world, Sigmund Freud and Ivan Pavlov had transformed our understanding of human behavior; Karl Marx's political and economic ideas were threatening the established order, industrialism was growing at a feverish pitch and the movies were here.

Into this dizzying vortex Meyerhold ran with open arms. Why, he thought, shouldn't the theater be a part of this new age? Why should it only reflect the trivia of everyday life? Wasn't the Russian documentary filmmaker Dziga Vertov right when he said, "The 'psychological' prevents man from being as precise as a stop-watch and hampers his desire for kinship with the machine"?[14] Wasn't Vertov also right when he called psychological drama "cine-vodka," stating that, "The film drama shrouds the eyes and brain in a sickly fog"?[15]

Meyerhold was looking for a revolution in the theater, a revolution for the actor. For his innovative production of *The Magnificent Cuckold,* he turned to artist and designer L. Popova. Popova provided a set unlike any other. It consisted of wooden scaffolding with ramps, slides and ladders attached. No conventional stage furniture could be found anywhere. The construction before the audience could be used as a boat, a house, a gymnasium, a kitchen, anything. It was the first use of a scenic design style which came to be known as, *Constructivism.*

In such a radical and revolutionary set, how were the actors to behave? What style would match the jagged angles and uneven playing levels? Of course, one look at such a set is all one needs to feel like a child in a playground. One simply wants to run up and jump on it. And that is just what the actors did.

Meyerhold realized that in order to break free of the restraints of realism, he must approach acting in a purely physical way. The road from the internal to the external was one Stanislavski had already mapped. His path must be different. He would travel from the external to the internal, from the surface to the core. He looked to the techniques of the Commedia del' arte, pantomime, the circus, and to the Kabuki and Noh theaters of Japan for inspiration.

From the Eastern theaters he learned about the importance of centers of gravity and so devised exercises based on the knees. At about the same time, it is interesting to note, Michael Chekhov was placing great importance on the feet as a building block of characterization. This importance of the feet and the lower extremities will come back later in the work of Tadashi Suzuki. From clowning he learned the power of the expressive mask, how the crying face and the laughing one can be combined and instantly alternated to create a sense of the grotesque. He learned from clowns the crucial elements of exaggeration and foolishness. From pantomime he learned how to create actors both strong and flexible and from the Commedia he learned how to create extended physical "lazzi" or "bits" that combined the skills of clowning and pantomime. The idea was to celebrate the theatrical, excite the audience and banish the world of the everyday.

Meyerhold felt that movement and gesture should be more important than words. This gave him license to rearrange text in any way he saw fit. He felt the actor should be an acrobat, a clown a trickster, capable of rapid transitions from one to the other. Meyerhold was in love with motion. And the symbol of motion in the modern age was the engine. The engine was at the heart of the machines that fascinated Meyerhold so. What was the actor's engine? His nervous system.

Meyerhold wanted to use the ideas of the American "efficiency expert" Frederick Taylor in the training of his new revolutionary actors. Taylor had analyzed the workers on an assembly line, discovering that they used many inefficient movements and gestures in the execution of their jobs. This efficiency of motion was of great interest to Meyerhold because he wanted to achieve the maximum effect on the audience in the most direct way possible.

Motion was the key to his new system. In one scene, Meyerhold had a man slide down an "S" shaped slide and arrive at the foot of his lover in order to express his joy and ecstasy at their meeting. Meyerhold felt this to be far more effective in conveying the emotion of the moment than any realistic staging might offer.

In his school, actors were "taught…to ignore in most instances subjective feelings, taught that the nucleus of expression is the action and reaction of the nerves and muscles, and transformed via exercises in boxing, tumbling, 'physical jerks,' running, jumping, dancing and climbing into alert, agile, functional men and women of the Communist regime."[16] It must be remembered that part of Meyerhold's dedication to revolution and Communism resulted from his rescue from the White Army by the Red Army during the Russian civil war.

Meyerhold felt that the realistic style created a theater of mood. That it put the audience under a kind of spell from which they were only freed after two or three hours. In the realistic theater, he thought, the spectators are dreaming away their time. But he wanted the audience to be awake, excited, and in the present. He wanted the audience to think about current political and social conditions and be aroused to action. He felt that properly presented physical actions could arouse emotion in audience members through reflex, and shock them into political and social insights that would remain with them after they left the auditorium.

The ideas of the Russian psychologist Ivan Pavlov suggested that through specific conditioning, behavior could be manipulated. If an actor comes down a slide with great glee shouting "wheee!" throughout the ride, the audience will share his exhilaration. The next time the actor mounts the slide, the audience will begin feeling the same exhilaration *before* the actor slides. They will have been conditioned to expect the feeling, and it will, reflexively, be there. This type of manipulation fascinated Meyerhold, and he needed actors physically capable of carrying out the actions he required.

In essence, Meyerhold rejected the idea of public solitude and the fourth wall. He expected the actor to be fully aware of the audience and to deliberately acknowledge and play for them. The Meyerhold actor was freed from the prison of natural behavior, but he paid a high price. His body had to submit to rigorous training and tremendous discipline. This training was accomplished through a technique that Meyerhold called, *Biomechanics.*

Just naming a few of the biomechanical exercises gives a taste of their essence: The Leap From the Back, The Horse and Rider, The Leap Onto the Chest, Dropping the Weight, Throwing the Stone, Shooting the Bow, The Slap in the Face, The Stab With the Dagger, Carrying the Sack and Strike With the Feet.

The first rule of this work is for the actor to find his center of balance, and the second rule is for the actor to find for his body an expressive position in space.[17] Let's examine one of these exercises.

Shooting the Bow: In this exercise a single actor moves through a series of twenty-four positions. He begins by falling to the floor onto one arm. (1) The other arm is extended behind him while both legs are stretched behind but bent at the knee. The actor then pulls his legs in, as the outstretched arm comes to rest against his side. (2) The actor then rises with his weight on his right foot and leans to his left shifting the weight to his left foot. (3-4) The right leg is now fairly straight while the left leg is bent. The right arm is now straight as though holding a bow. The left arm is bent as it begins to draw up the bow. The actor then comes forward. (5-6) He then sees a target, shifting his weight from one side to the other. (7-10) He then reaches behind him and takes out an imaginary arrow from a crouching position. (11) The actor then straightens his legs placing the left about two to three feet in front of the right. He bends his torso so that it is at a 90° angle to his left leg. Both arms are also straight with the left arm reaching to the ankle of the left leg, and the right arm stretched out 180° from the left one. (12)

Now the actor bends his knees as his torso comes up and he places an arrow in the imaginary string of the bow. (13) He then pulls the arrow back with his right hand coming just below his chin. He then releases the arrow, the right arm coming forward to join the left. (14-15) He thrusts his right arm straight down and raises his left elbow up above his head, bends his knees forward bringing both arms up together, curves his upper body over to the right and then thrusts the right arm straight down in 180° opposition to his left arm. (16-18)

Meyerhold: Shooting the Bow

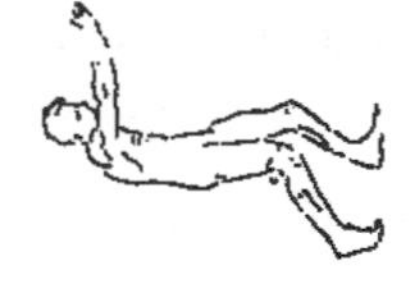

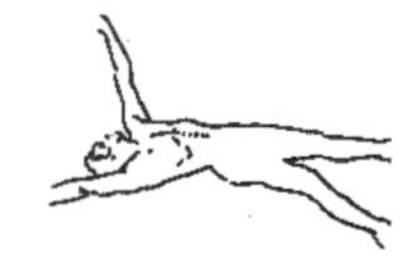

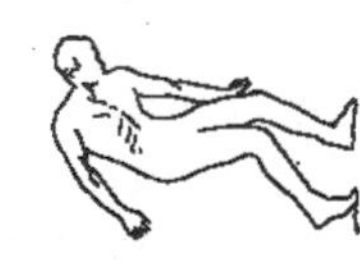

This exercise is quite physically demanding. Try it. Remember that the positions are not held for long. They are "flowed through." Yet the actor should be capable of holding each one if asked. This exercise calls for strength and balance and helps make the actor become aware of shifting centers of gravity.

But more importantly, it demonstrates the cycle of acting that Meyerhold felt was fundamental to his work: *Intention* (to shoot an arrow at a target), *Realization* (actually releasing the arrow from the bow) and *Refusal of the Action* (the body contractions after the arrow has been fired).[18] The influence of Stanislavski is clear. Meyerhold's "intention" is like Stanislavski's "objective," and his "realization" is like Stanislavski's "action." The "refusal of the action" is really the reaction to the action as seen in the body; the release of the arrow causing the body to recoil in opposition.

Training in biomechanics created a physically flexible and responsive actor, but the exercises themselves were not to be seen in performance, they were for use only in the studio. On stage, the physicality of the actor was put to use in innovative productions designed to satirize middle-class life, and to propagandize for the new Communist way. But when the new policy of "Socialist Realism" was instituted in the 1930's, Meyerhold's bold spirit was stifled. The new policy called for art forms that the common man could understand and condemned as "anti-Soviet" almost all experimental and avant-garde forms in the arts. When Meyerhold criticized the inhibiting effects of this new policy, he was arrested and sent into exile, where he died in 1942.

It must be said that his biomechanical ideas never constituted a complete system in the Stanislavski sense. He was vague about it, and wrote very little to explain it. His system produced few actors of international stature, but became an inspiration for many actors and directors after him who also felt constrained by the boundaries of realism. And while Meyerhold's productions were theatrical in the highest sense, Vakhtangov ultimately found them devoid of true feeling.

While Meyerhold abandoned realistic theater, he never renounced Stanislavski. Two years before his death, he proclaimed himself still a student of that great man. And what did Stanislavski feel for this man who had drifted so far from him in his work? Just before he died, Stanislavski declared "Take care of Meyerhold; he is my only heir in the theater—here or anywhere else."[19]

Was Meyerhold completely against the expression of emotion? No. But he was not interested in the theater of personal feeling. Emotion, he felt, came from actions, and when it did, it was appropriate. But he did not want his actors to be overcome by feeling, to indulge its presence, or to reveal private emotion in public. The actor was at all times to be in control of both his body and his feelings. Emotions were not necessarily to be felt, but only shown.

Meyerhold's approach to the arousal of feeling was completely from the outside. He stands in a tradition stretching from Quintilian through Aaron Hill to Delsarte. Yet he went beyond them. Even they were concerned with the expression of authentic feeling in the actor. Meyerhold was not. He was more concerned with the creation of feeling in the audience itself. This crucial difference marks out Meyerhold as a true innovator whose work stands as a beacon for those primarily interested in the theater's effect upon the spectator. The great Russian filmmaker Sergei Eisenstein (who was Meyerhold's assistant for two years), the German playwright and director Bertolt Brecht, the Polish director Jerzy Grotowski, and countless others have been influenced by Meyerhold in this way.

❄

Evgeni Vakhtangov, Michael Chekhov and Vsevolod Meyerhold. Three artistic children of Constantine Stanislavski. Individuals as different from each other as they were from their artistic father. But even as they extended, challenged and rejected his ideas, their love for the man and his accomplishments never wavered. And no matter the disagreements, Stanislavski loved them back. After all, hadn't he, as a young man, rejected the training of the Imperial Dramatic School in order to retain his own sense of uniqueness? Weren't these men driven by their unique artistic passions? Stanislavski's spirit was a huge one, and his embrace was wide. And that embrace was lovingly returned by the three men who were inspired to their greatest artistic achievements by him. Together, these four tireless workers and visionaries created the modern style of acting.

Chapter 4

The American Revolution

On December 27th, 1922, the *RMS Majestic* set sail from France. On board were the members of the Moscow Art Theater, headed for the first time to America. The MAT was scheduled to tour the United States for nearly a year and a half, performing in New York, Brooklyn, Newark, Boston, Philadelphia, Pittsburg, Cleveland, Chicago and Detroit. After nine difficult days at sea, they landed in New York City. When they left in the spring of 1924, they had forever changed the American theatrical landscape.

The theater the MAT found in New York was one dominated by commercial Broadway productions featuring "star" players such as John Barrymore, Katherine Cornell, Helen Hayes, and Alfred Lunt. Minor parts were of little interest to the producers of these star vehicles and were therefore often performed by actors of indifferent ability. But there was other theater to be discovered as well.

In reaction to the Broadway state of affairs, some alternative theater groups had sprung up. The Neighborhood Playhouse was one of these, as was The Washington Square Players. Another, The Provincetown Playhouse, was the first to produce the work of Eugene

O'Neill. In 1919, The Washington Square Players became The Theater Guild, whose aim was to produce great plays with great actors for commercial profit. They had a school, a permanent company and tremendous prestige and success. Another alternative to the Broadway "star" theater was provided by Eva Le Gallienne at her Civic Repertory Theater. There, she produced the great classic plays, and provided training for young actors.

But when the MAT performed *Tsar Fyodor* at the Jolson Theater on January 8, 1923, *The Lower Depths,* on the 15th and *The Cherry Orchard* on the 26th, no one in America had ever seen anything like it. Every actor, no matter how small the role, was brilliant. The depth of feeling and the detail of the actor's work startled and amazed the critics and public alike. Nothing the Theater Guild had ever done, nothing on Broadway, equaled the impact of Stanislavski's company. In city after city, actors, critics and the general public were astonished at the artistry of the Moscow Art Theater. Curiosity about the Stanislavski system was overwhelming. Richard Boleslavsky, a member of the MAT who had come to America by himself in 1922, wrote an article for a theater magazine on the system to satisfy this demand.

But he knew this would not be enough. People didn't want just articles, they wanted to know what the Russians knew; the Stanislavski system. So with the aid of MAT actress Maria Ouspenskaya, he opened a school for actors at 139 MacDougal Street in New York City and called it The American Lab Theater. It was here, at the Lab, that the Russian revolution gained its lasting foothold. Finally, Americans could learn to do what they saw the Russians doing.

And what, in fact, were the Russians doing? What must a Moscow Art Theater production have been like to see? Unlike film, theater is transitory, so when it's over, it's over. And yet, we like to think that we can get a glimpse of the extraordinary individual and ensemble acting that characterized the MAT at its best by watching Jan Kadar's 1965 Czechoslovakian film, *The Shop On Main Street.* One scene in particular epitomizes for me what it seems the MAT was doing. Go ahead and rent the movie. Better yet, if you can afford it, buy the movie, it bears close study. The scene I refer to is the one wherein the lead character Tono and his wife host a dinner for his wife's sister and her husband. The complex emotional and physically expressive detail of the actors cannot help but remind us of what we have read of the Moscow Art Theater at its height. The actors create deep and rich individual characters and interact with each other with all of the spontaneity, humor, and complexity of a true "ensemble of stars." Sometimes, watching this scene, we feel that we are catching a glimpse, back through time, of that revolutionary theater that changed forever the face of drama.

❄

The appearances of the Moscow Art Theater in the United States inspired many young actors to dedicate themselves to a new kind of theater. Among them was the man who was soon to transform "The System," into "The Method."

Lee Strasberg came to America from Eastern Europe in 1901. As a young man he joined a dramatics club at the Chrystie Street Settlement House, where he won an award for his acting. While there, he read many of the most important books and articles on theater and found his imagination and passions on fire. He went to see the greatest actors of his time, and hoped to understand how they achieved what they did. When he heard about Boleslavsky's Lab Theater, he did not hesitate to sign up. It was there that he was taught the essence of Stanislavski's ideas and trained in their practical use.

And here, we must step back. It is crucial to remember that Stanislavski's notions about acting were constantly changing. So what the students of the American Lab were taught were not the ideas that Stanislavski evolved after 1920 or so. In addition, the work of Vakhtangov had a strong influence on Boleslavsky and informed much of his teaching. So what did the Lab teach, we wonder?

Boleslavsky taught mainly by lecturing on various aspects of the system, while Ouspenskaya taught the exercises and did the scene work. Later, Boleslavsky also began teaching directing to advanced students. Classes were also available in movement and voice. In short, the Lab attempted a total approach to the training of an actor.

Ouspenskaya put great emphasis on concentration and relaxation, as Strasberg was to do some years later himself. She gave the students improvisations which involved the exploration of given circumstances, sense memory and emotion memory. This last, was given tremendous importance. The creation of true emotion was at the heart of the training. Strasberg had read Ribot's *Psychology of the Emotions,* as had Stanislavski, of course, and knew of the idea that emotions could be recalled by an actor and used in a part. Ribot called this emotion memory, *"affective memory,"* and both Boleslavsky and Ouspenskaya put great emphasis on it. "Ouspenskaya," says Strasberg, "used to call the actor's affective memories 'golden keys' which unlocked some of the greatest moments in acting."[1]

Ouspenskaya also used animal exercises to help actors to characterize. Actors were to closely observe animal behavior at home or at the zoo and imitate it in class. Actors had to walk and move like the animal, eat like the animal, be like the animal. The purpose was twofold; to enhance each actor's powers of observation and concentration, and to give them new ways of moving and using their bodies. They had to become aware of the different centers of gravity in each animal, of the tempo-rhythms of each creature, of their responses to surprise, to food, to others of their kind, and to people.

The other great key that Boleslavsky gave to the students on MacDougal street was Vakhtangov's reformulation of Stanislavski's "magic if." Remember, Stanislavski used "if" like this: If I were this character, how would I act? If I were in this circumstance, how would I behave? Vakhtangov made a significant alteration to Stanislavski's questions. He posed them this way: "How do I motivate myself, or what would have to motivate me, to behave as the character behaves?"[2]

What is so important about this change? Isn't it really just a matter of semantics, of using different words to say the same thing? Not really. Vakhtangov's "adjustment" allows the actor to roam outside the boundaries of the play for help. If the circumstances in the play do not stimulate an actor to the proper behavior or feeling, she can go beyond the play and use anything that gets her to the right place.

If she is supposed to show great love and tenderness for a picture she holds of the character's daughter, she may find herself able to accomplish her task better by substituting her own daughter's picture in the frame. Or by simply imagining her own daughter in the frame. Or perhaps by using a mental or literal picture of herself as a young girl. This becomes the actor's secret. No one need know.

In fact, if you combine Vakhtangov's adjustment with affective memory, you have a powerful tool for eliciting emotion in yourself. If you must express great grief in a scene, and it just isn't there, recalling a tragic moment in your own life may bring you to the proper place. And no one would be the wiser. No one would know that you were not playing the circumstance of the scene. The effect would be the same. Or would it? A part of us rebels at this. Isn't it really a way of cheating? Doesn't doing this pull us out of the play? Isn't it a kind of deception? Do the means justify the ends in acting? We'll return to these questions later, when we examine Lee Strasberg and the Method in more detail.

The training at the Lab was to last two years. The first year, mostly with Madame Ouspenskaya, covered given circumstances, characterization and affective memory. In the second year, "Boleslavsky analyzed a play according to its spine, mood, and beats. Actors were taught to analyze their roles according to their characters' desires and intentions..."[3] In other words, the first year was spent mostly on the actor himself, and the second on his approach to the role. By "spine," Boleslavsky meant the super-objective and the through-line of action the actor follows to achieve it.

Strasberg left the Lab after the first year. And one can only wonder if his subsequent methods of teaching would have been different had he stayed on for that second year of study. In years to come, he will be severely criticized for putting too little emphasis on "actions" and too much on emotional expression. But that is in the future.

And what of the future of the American theater? Many felt that it would not find its true expression through the work of the Russian expatriates at the Lab. They longed to create a Stanislavski-based theater that had an American accent. And three did something about it.

In May of 1930, twenty-seven actors and three others set out to rehearse in a barn in Connecticut and create the Moscow Art Theater-American style.

For years, the young Harold Clurman had been giving talks in New York to anyone who would listen about a new American theater. He had been overwhelmed by the MAT's performances in the U.S., and been influenced in Paris by the great Jacques Copeau and his theater. He spoke about the lack of unity in the current American theatrical scene. Each actor, he felt, was a hired gun, who worked from production to production, with no overriding purpose other than to play each part well. Clurman demanded more than this. He wanted a theater that produced new American works presented by a permanent company dedicated to "the essential moral and social preoccupation's of our time."[4] Who came to listen? Many actors who knew something of Stanislavski, and some who didn't. Artists from all disciplines came to hear this dynamic speaker paint a verbal picture of an American arts scene that many had dreamed of but few pursued. He wanted all artists to focus on the problems of the society to which they belonged, and to lend their creative spirits to creating a community with the public. The theater specifically, he felt, needed a single vision, and actors needed a common vocabulary and purpose. This, he said, could only be supplied by the study and application of the ideas of Stanislavski. His was a clarion call to those out-of-work actors suffering under the Depression and the star theater of Broadway.

In his effort to arouse artists to his side, he was helped by two other people: Cheryl Crawford, and Lee Strasberg. Together, these three would forge, from many different sources, the most important and influential theater in America.

Before the start of The Group Theater's first season, they retreated to a barn and some houses outside Danbury, Connecticut. Here, they would form a company and rehearse their first production; Paul Green's, *The House of Connelly.*

The acting members and three founders came from diverse cultures, ethnic groups, social strata, and possessed various degrees of theatrical experience. Clurman was a cultural sophisticate who attended Columbia for a time, lived in Paris for a while, and whose father was a doctor. Crawford came from a wealthy family and attended Smith College. Strasberg came to America at the age of seven. He lived on the lower East Side with his family and was destined to be in the wig business until acting captured his attention. Three very different people who, for a time, complemented each others strengths and weaknesses to perfection.

Among the actors, the situation was the same. Stella Adler, whom Clurman and Strasberg met at the Actor's Lab, was already an established actress in the vital Yiddish theater. Her father, Jacob Adler, was one of the finest actors of his generation and one whom Strasberg regarded highly. Sometimes, to her, the members of the Group seemed like rank amateurs. But she believed in the ideals of the Group and stayed with it for many years. Harold Clurman was soon to fall deeply in love with her. Another actor with an already established reputation was Morris Carnovsky. He had acted with both the Provincetown Players and the Theater Guild but felt that his acting needed more emotional depth. Another original member was Franchot Tone. A young leading actor who would always be torn between the seriousness of the Group, and the glamour of Hollywood. Eunice Stoddard was a literate New Yorker whose father was a lawyer. Carnovsky brought in J. Edward Bromberg, Robert Lewis talked his way in, Sanford Meisner was a friend of Strasberg's and Clurman's, and Clifford Odets impressed Clurman with his passion and humor. Altogether this group of thirty consisted of lower, middle, and upper-class people, immigrant, and native born Americans, and acting novices and experts. Creating unity from so much diversity was the daunting task facing Clurman, Crawford and Strasberg in their first summer together. How could it be done?

Clurman talked. And when Clurman talked everyone could meet at the place of his vision. Part of the unity that the Group achieved was due in no small part to Clurman's ability to keep their eyes on their larger purpose. No matter what rancor might occur during rehearsals, Clurman could patch it up with a speech. His eloquence kept them on track. But more was needed than talk. Unity must be achieved in another, more specific way. And this job fell to Lee Strasberg. Clurman had been impressed by the way Strasberg used what he had learned at the Lab in some of his directing at The Chrystie Street Settlement, and felt that Strasberg should direct the first Group production. Strasberg accepted the assignment but realized that more than conventional directing would be required. Teaching was needed as well.

The factor that would cement the group together was the Stanislavski system. Each of the acting members needed to be schooled in the techniques discovered by Stanislavski and Vakhtangov if they were to achieve the sense of ensemble playing and inner truth to which they were all dedicated. And this is what Strasberg did. Each day, Clurman would lecture on some aspect of theater history or practice, and Strasberg would teach the system and rehearse the play.

Strasberg called what he taught a "method." It was compounded of Stanislavski, Vakhtangov and other ideas taken from his voluminous reading. He did exercises designed to increase the actors' concentration. For example, they were asked to observe an object for three minutes, after which time, it would be removed from the field of view. The actor was then asked to describe it. Many of them failed to see details, to recall textures, shapes or weight. But the more they did this exercise, the better and more keenly they learned to observe and evaluate what was in front of them. They then moved on to imaginary objects, "enacting the slicing and eating of an apple, the drinking of a glass of tea, picking up pearls or nuts from the floor and showing by the movements of their fingers, which was which."[5] This of course enlarged their use of the imagination and gave the actors some experience with sense memory.

They used improvisation, as both Stanislavski and Vakhtangov had, when working on scenes from the play. They would create situations implied by the text and do them. Suppose they were doing *The Cherry Orchard* by Anton Chekhov. Since the characters have grown up with this orchard behind their house, the actors might improvise a picnic in it. They might imagine themselves as children putting up a swing on one of the large branches. They might improvise a scene wherein one of them was injured by a fall from the swing. How would they react? What would they do? This is a technique that creates a history between the actors and usually manifests itself onstage as a greater connection between the members of the cast.

They also did improvisations based on scenes explicitly in the play. They would play the given circumstances of the scene, but not use the writer's words. In this way, they were able to "respond honestly and spontaneously"[6] to the situation. After a while, the author's text was used. But the main technique that Strasberg insisted upon using was affective memory.

The idea was to use the remembered feelings of the actor and express them through the character on the stage. Strasberg's specific technique of doing this will be discussed more fully in the section on him. For now, it is enough to know that at appropriate moments in the play, ones that called for strong emotion, the actors would do an affective memory exercise and then speak their lines or do their actions from the newly aroused emotional state.

It was these exercises in affective memory that so impressed the members of the Group, that they came to regard Strasberg as their most important leader. They felt that they were reaching new areas of emotional truth and expression in their acting and they were overjoyed. Strasberg pushed them beyond what was theatrically acceptable, and personally comfortable. He would not settle for clichéd responses, but insisted that they dig deeper into themselves and break through the barriers that kept them from revealing their deepest feelings. He knew it was fear inducing work, but the results seemed worth the efforts.

When *The House Of Connelly* opened in New York in September of 1931, the company received sixteen curtain calls. One critic wrote, "I cannot remember a more completely consecrated piece of work since the Moscow Art masters went home."[7] The Group had succeeded. Over one remarkable summer, they had created a company of superb individual actors who played with each other with the ensemble feeling of a family.

But as with all families, conflicts abounded. One actress complained about the affective memory exercises. In a scene with a fellow player, she noticed him dropping out of his connection with her and going inside of himself in order to "do an exercise." When she complained to Strasberg about this, he told her that she needed to do more of what the offending actor was doing. Others also had their problem with emotion memory. Robert Lewis, Sanford Meisner and Stella Adler all were uncomfortable with it, although they realized its value. They felt that it limited their acting style to a form of extreme realism and was perhaps not so useful for stylized plays with heightened prose styles, such as the works of Shakespeare. After some years Carnovsky as well felt that he was simply repeating himself. Others felt that they were running out of personal experiences to mine. Strasberg however, felt that they were resisting exploring parts of their psyche of which they were afraid.

Cheryl Crawford was dissatisfied with her role as the practical one. When money needed to be raised, they turned to her. But when a director was needed, they passed her over. Her resentment grew. The players became suspicious of Clurman's talk because he never directed anything. Among the players themselves there was division. Some actors got bigger parts more consistently than others, and the rules did not seem to apply equally to all. Because Clurman and Adler were living together, some felt that she received special treatment. Irritations smoldered.

But over the next few years these hotbeds of discontent were held in check and did not burst into flames. Each summer they went on retreat to work on a play and continue studying. They took classes in movement and in voice. New members were admitted and became a source of great strength. Among them was the man who would later co-found the Actor's Studio, Elia Kazan. Others included John (Jules) Garfield and Francis Farmer.

Strasberg began using improvisation more. In one exercise, he asked the actors to improvise on a single word. In one case the word was "liberty." "One actress interpreted 'liberty' as the Statue of Liberty, whose arm began to waver as her torch turned into a cocktail glass and she lowered it to her lips; the exercise ended with Miss Liberty getting drunk."[8] Exercises like this freed the actors' imaginations and injected some much needed humor into the proceedings.

Some of these improvisations were so successful that the actors would do them at benefit shows to raise money.

Over the next three years, Group productions alternated between successes and failures. One of the successes was a play called *Men In White.* The center piece of this play is a hospital operation. Strasberg and the actors worked painstakingly to create a powerfully theatrical view of the heroic actions of doctors at work. The lighting was stark and dramatic and the actors' actions were choreographed with incredible attention to detail. Here was the Group and Strasberg reaching beyond the realism of *The House of Connelly,* and embracing the theatricalism of Vakhtangov.

How did they do it? At first they were led astray by an over reliance on the emotional life of the doctors and nurses. As they performed the operation scene in rehearsals, the actors showed their deep emotional responses to the emergency.

But they all knew something was wrong. The scene wasn't playing correctly. It was the insight of Cheryl Crawford that gave them the key. These health professionals would not be caught up in their emotional lives during an operation. They would, in fact, be doing what they had been trained to do. They would proceed with skill and concentration not allowing their personal feelings to intrude. This proved to be the crucial adjustment.

When *Men In White* opened, it overwhelmed both audiences and critics. It gave the Group some financial success and garnered the first real public recognition of Strasberg's talents as a director. The Group was stretching itself beyond realism with the same techniques it used from its inception. Some began to realize that theatricalism and the Stanislavski system were not mutually exclusive.

One year later all hell broke loose. On July 3, 1934, Stella Adler met Constantine Stanislavski in Paris. He was there recuperating from an illness and she had been traveling in the Soviet Union with Clurman observing the various theaters there. When Adler and Clurman learned that the man who created the system they were using was in Paris, they decided to visit him.

At the time, Adler was having a very difficult time rehearsing a role in the Group's newest production, *Gentlewoman.* She was beginning to resent Strasberg's directorial methods and she was having trouble with the technique of affective memory. After awhile she finally spoke to Stanislavski.

She told him that he had destroyed acting for her. That once it had been a source of great joy to her, but that now she hated it. And she blamed his system for this change. Stanislavski told her that if her love of acting had been shattered, then the system was not for her. That she should not use it. Perhaps, he suggested, the problem was that she was not using the system correctly. She began to tell him what they were doing at the Group Theater. When she described the exercises in affective memory, Stanislavski broke in. He told her that he had abandoned such work years earlier because he found that it led to hysteria in the actors. He said that actors should not dig for emotions, but play actions and live in the circumstances of the play. He asked her if she would like to work with him on her part from *Gentlewoman.* She said yes. Wouldn't you? For six weeks they met every day and worked for hours. For Adler, it was a revelation. She couldn't wait to get back to the Group and tell them where they had gone wrong.

Strasberg had learned the system from Boleslavsky and Ouspenskaya, and the system they learned was Stanislavski's up to the time they left Moscow for the United States. But his ideas had changed, and they were unaware of this. Stanislavski had moved on to his *Method of Psycho-Physical Actions,* which emphasized actions and circumstances far more than emotion memory.

Adler was overjoyed. She had noticed difficulties with actor's taking a minute onstage to prepare for an emotional moment, and questioned its true effectiveness. The way it worked was this. About a minute before an emotional moment arrived in a scene, the actor would begin doing an affective memory exercise to produce the required feeling.

Now during that minute the actor still had to respond to the other actors on the stage, be aware of his cues, execute his actions and be present in the moment. This is a very difficult thing to do. Actors would notice other actors checking in and checking out; being present one moment, and absent the next. And yet for some, it produced exciting and honest results. For others, however, it created problems.

Stanislavski said there was a better way. Emotions, he told Adler, cannot be commanded to appear. And they should not be directly assaulted. The best way to achieve the truest expression of the emotion of the character, he said, was to follow the through-line of the character's actions and to let the emotions come from that. If the actor enters the circumstances of the play with commitment and belief, the actions will stimulate the proper feelings.

Stanislavski emphasized *communion* (p.53) in his work. Meaning by this not only the actor's contact with the audience, but the actor's communication with the other actors. Affective memory exercises, when used during the performance of a play, interfered with this vital connection.

Adler's assistant took extensive notes and she brought back with her a chart detailing Stanislavski's system. In August of 1934 she began giving a series of talks to the Group at their summer retreat.

Now it must be said that the ideas she brought back from Paris are controversial. Some believe that Stanislavski was sick and perhaps not in his clearest mind. Others maintain that confronted by what he referred to as an hysterical actress, he played down the emotional aspects of his work. And yet, when one hears what the later members of the Art Theater say about Stanislavski's changes to his system, they concur with what Adler told the Group.

When Adler addressed The Group, Strasberg was noticeably absent. Strasberg felt that Stanislavski had gone back on himself, and he felt betrayed. He was no longer the only expert on the Stanislavski system, and he didn't like this. Strasberg was very attached to affective memory and its uses and was not about to give it up. Hadn't it brought the Group some of their greatest successes? Hadn't the members sworn by it in their first summer together? Strasberg told other members that the productions he had seen at the Moscow Art Theater in the thirties were tired and bland. He felt himself closer to

Vakhtangov than to Stanislavski. He didn't know that Stanislavski too was worried about the decline of the MAT, and felt that it no longer represented the best working out of his ideas.

Members like Robert Lewis and Sanford Meisner found Adler's talks inspiring. "You could feel the fog lifting as she went from one technical point to another...We were all so oppressed by this over-usage of emotion memory."[9] "More important than our apparent misuse of emotion memory was the fact that we were using circumstances from our own lives. What Stella told us was that Stanislavski concentrated on the circumstances in the play...Until then the Group had always worked from sense memory but never from given circumstances."[10] The members of the Group began to feel independent of Strasberg. His iron grip had been loosened.

Adler began teaching some very popular and effective classes and Odets, Meisner and Kazan went to work on a short play to which they all contributed. Late in 1935, Odets put this new play in final form and read it to the other members of the Group. It is interesting to note that this first reading took place in a theater named the Majestic. In a sense, the ship *Majestic* that had brought the Moscow Art Theater to America, found its most important port in this Boston building. The play that Odets read in the basement of the Majestic Theater was *Waiting For Lefty*, the play that was to become most identified with the Group Theater. The play was co-directed by Odets and Meisner and created such a sensation, that theaters all over the country were desperate to produce it.

Waiting For Lefty was everything that Clurman had promised. It examined both personal and social issues in so explosive a way that people felt their lives changed after having seen it. The play reveals, in a series of short scenes, how different workers come to agree upon a worker strike. The writing was brilliant and biting and the acting, inspired. And it was all done without Strasberg. Strasberg was, in fact, hostile to Odets' writing and didn't direct any of his plays for years. It must be admitted, however, that Strasberg had trained all of the actors and a part of their success was certainly due to his efforts.

Another Odets play brought the Group more success and marked the directorial debut of Harold Clurman. *Awake And Sing* was rehearsed in an atmosphere of joy and discovery. Clurman did not insist on affective memory exercises, but encouraged the actor's imaginations and trusted their judgments. On opening night, the play and acting ensemble received fifteen curtain calls. Stella Adler's performance was singled out for praise as was the work of her brother Luther Adler, Morris Carnovsky, and Sanford Meisner. Adler's new understanding of the Stanislavski system had a tremendous impact on her. She worked with a renewed sense of joy, concentration, and finesse. The whole company felt that they were working at their highest level. *Waiting For Lefty* and *Awake And Sing* gave the Group a sense of their own power and maturity. They no longer felt that Strasberg had all the answers. Some members even began teaching outside of the Group itself.

They even looked outside of the Group for acting teachers. In 1935, Michael Chekhov was in New York, and the Group wanted very much to meet him. Again Strasberg was not happy about this. But many members had been so impressed by his acting that they wanted to learn from him. Unfortunately, they concluded that his style was so personal to him that it could not really be taught or used by others. In this, they were probably mistaken. It was an historic opportunity that was left unrealized.

By 1936 The Group Theater was the most respected and admired theater in the country. Smaller theaters in other cities looked up to them as the heroes of the new drama. In Chicago, Cleveland, Boston, Detroit, and Los Angeles, theater talk often turned to The Group. Everyone wanted to be a part of it. And for awhile, even Bertold Brecht's musical collaborator Kurt Weill found himself there. Yes, Kurt Weill taught musical theater to members of The Group at their theater. For a short period of time two great lines of dramatic performance, the Stanislavskian and the Brechtian merged. They missed Michael Chekhov, but they got some Brecht.

The Group had one more astonishing success in Odets' play *Golden Boy*, but by 1939 both Crawford and Strasberg had resigned their memberships in The Group, and the actors were no longer feeling challenged. By 1941, The Group was finished. The members scattered to different jobs and new careers. Kazan began directing more regularly in both New York and Hollywood, Lewis and Strasberg continued to direct in the theater, and Carnovsky, Adler and Meisner went into teaching.

What had been a group, was now just a scattering of individuals. Together they created the most celebrated American theater of the twentieth century. The Moscow Art Theater had Anton Chekhov, The Group had Clifford Odets. The Moscow Art Theater had Stanislavski and Danchenko, and The Group had Strasberg and Clurman. It is the highest tribute to the achievements of The Group Theater that their work can be spoken of in the same breath as The Moscow Art Theater. They did what they set out to do. Many theaters have started with high ideals, the Group Theater met them.

Much of actor training in the United States today came out of the Group experience. We will examine this legacy by probing the ideas and teaching of former Group members, Lee Strasberg, Stella Adler, and Sanford Meisner. Along with Kazan, Clurman, and Lewis, they put the ideas of Stanislavski at the center of the American actor's map.

Chapter 5

Lee Strasberg

So, here we are. At THE METHOD. Over the years, a man, a place, and a technique have become synonymous; Lee Strasberg, The Actor's Studio and The Method. In fact, the formula in most people's minds is this: Lee Strasberg + The Method + the Actor's Studio= Marlon Brando, acting genius. But that equation is hopelessly misleading, and so, before we discuss Strasberg's ideas in detail, we need to dispel a few myths.

First, Marlon Brando. Here is what he has to say in his 1994 autobiography about the man presumed by most to be his teacher: "Lee Strasberg tried to take credit for teaching me how to act. He never taught me anything...To me he was a tasteless and untalented person...I went to the Actor's Studio...because of Elia Kazan...But Strasberg never taught me acting. Stella (Adler) did—and Kazan."[1] The truth is that Brando had been a student of Stella Adler's at the New School For Social Research before he ever set foot in the Actor's Studio. So the man most associated in the public's mind with The Method, never studied with Lee Strasberg. The slouching posture and mumbling speech for which Brando has from time to time been criticized, does not result from any method that he learned from

Strasberg. It also does not result from his work with Adler or Kazan. It is simply Brando.

The second myth has to do with the Actor's Studio itself. Lee Strasberg was not a founding member of that famous institution, and it's initial fame did not stem from his involvement with it.

The Actor's Studio was co-founded by Elia Kazan, Robert Lewis and Cheryl Crawford in 1947. Crawford acted as the business director, while Kazan taught a beginning class, and Lewis an advanced one.

Under Kazan and Lewis, the work at the studio embraced a greater sense of theatricality then it was to do under Strasberg's guidance. Kazan in fact could be said to stand in relation to Strasberg, as Vakhtangov stood to Stanislavski.

People initially came to the Studio because of the directing successes of Lewis and Kazan and because each of the founders had been a member of the famous Group Theater. Strasberg did not exercise any significant influence over the Studio until four years after its creation.

❄

It is safe to say that Lee Strasberg's teachings have stirred up more passionate controversy than any other acting teacher's in the United States. Some maintain that he is responsible for training and helping many of the finest actors and actresses in this country. Others contend that his methods have ruined an entire generation of performers. Nothing else stirs up the feelings of actors, directors and teachers like the name "Strasberg," or the style known as the "Method."

What is The Method, anyway? It is a version of the Stanislavski system that puts the greatest emphasis on the creation of an inner technique that enables an actor to express deep feeling whenever he needs it. In popular understanding, the method is Strasberg's creation. And although what Robert Lewis, Sanford Meisner, and Stella Adler teach is also a version of the Stanislavski system, it is Strasberg's version that has become known as The Method.

When the young Lee Strasberg read Gordon Craig's 1911 book, *On The Art of the Theater,* he was stunned. In this book, Craig maintains that acting is not an art at all. In acting, he says, feelings are more important than thought and because emotions are uncontrollable, they are not exactly repeatable night after night. This inability of the actor to repeat and control his performance perfectly makes his profession inartistic. Great acting, Craig stated, is largely accidental. Because of this, he would prefer to do away with the actor and replace him with what he calls the *Über-marionette.* This marionette would be controllable by the director, and be able to execute perfectly any demand, performance after performance. This, of course, is a startling statement. And Strasberg began to wonder if Craig was right. If an actor had no way of achieving the same level of expression night after night, if he had no control over the level and degree of his emotional expression, could what he does be properly called an art?

When he saw the Moscow Art Theater perform in New York, he realized that it was possible for actors to be artists. He saw these extraordinary Russian actors repeat high emotion from performance to performance, and he was determined to find out how it was done. Craig could be proved wrong, and Strasberg was determined to provide that proof.

When he learned from Boleslavsky and Ouspenskaya the technique of affective memory, he felt he had found the key that would open the door to controllable emotion. And over the course of the years, when others questioned the true value of emotion memory, he staunchly defended it and even widened its use. He felt that affective memory was the very heart and soul of Stanislavski's and Vakhtangov's systems and he was fiercely dedicated to it. If he was wrong, it meant that Craig was right, and that human actors were incapable of being true artists. And this was a position that Strasberg could not tolerate. In some ways, the rest of his life can be seen as an attempt to show that Craig was mistaken and to prove beyond doubt that acting is as high an art as any other. We might, if we were feeling bold, call this Lee Strasberg's *Super-objective.* It is perhaps why he fought so hard against its detractors.

What Strasberg did not seem to question was the validity of Craig's views. Craig's call for perfection makes the actor more of a machine than a human. He asks not only for the impossible, but denies the value of spontaneity. Certainly an actor must come extremely close each night to the same performance levels, but to demand perfect reproduction is to devalue the small variations which often give vitality and life to a performance. An element of unpredictability is part of the actor's art. On the other hand, it is easy to sympathize with Craig when one sees performances that differ wildly in quality night after night. But Craig's call for *Über-marionettes* is absurd. Although he may soon get his wish.

The technology of the late twentieth century makes it possible to create synthetic actors via the use of computers. A perfectly realistic digital body can be created and made to move realistically across a computer screen speaking realistic dialogue created by means of synthetic speech programs which can all be precisely controlled by a program designer. Thus, Craig's *Über-marionette* is well within reach.

The idea is frightening isn't it? It threatens the very existence of human actors. This is how Strasberg must have felt when he read Craig's book.

Strasberg set out to create an actor who was truly an artist and who could not be replaced.

❄

The beginning of training in Strasberg's Method is relaxation. He realized, along with Delsarte and Stanislavski, that bodily tension can lead to expressive restriction. Tension keeps the actor from doing what he wants to do. His voice becomes thin rather than full, his body becomes stiff rather than pliant, his mind becomes rigid instead of flexible and his emotions become frozen rather than yielding.

RELAXATION

The actor new to Strasberg's work always begins with relaxation exercises. The student is asked to sit in a chair, and to find a position in which he might be able to fall asleep. Falling asleep, however, is not the goal, so the chair should not be one that is too comfortable.

Next, the student is asked to concentrate on various muscle groups and to consciously release any tension being held there. Often the student is guided to begin with the feet. The foot is our first connection with a surface beyond our body, and is asked to support the bulk of our weight. The numerous subtle adjustments that our feet and ankles go through just to keep us balanced and moving, puts tremendous strain on them. Moving the ankles and toes slowly can be helpful in getting them to release. Try it. Rotate your feet slowly at the ankles, flex and curl your toes now as you read.

Slowly, we work our way through the body, concentrating in turn on the calves, the upper legs, the mid-section, the buttocks, our fingers, wrists, lower and upper arms, shoulders, chest, neck, lips, and eyes.

We keep in mind that Strasberg paid special attention to three areas. One, is the side of the temples: "In the effort we make to think, these areas use much more energy than they need, and therefore create tension."[2] Imagine how good it would feel to have strong but gentle fingers massaging our temples right now. We close our eyes and just let the tension pour out of our temples into the air. Some of our thoughts are heavy and they sink to the ground. Others drift upwards and disappear.

We suddenly realize that our teeth are clenched, and we slowly release our jaw muscles. Tension, we see, creeps in on cat's paws; subtly and without warning. Again we focus on relaxing the temples. This time we meet with more success.

Next, we focus on the bridge of the nose. Muscles from there lead to the eyes, and because our eyes are in motion so much of the time, tension builds up there. We realize that the "look" of concentration that we put on our face when we're listening to someone, is really just habitual. We think we appear thoughtful when we pinch our eyebrows inward and scrunch up the muscles between our eyes. But this look of "concern" is simply a mask we have been putting on for years. We have a surprising amount of difficulty letting these small muscle groups go. But when we do, we feel something almost miraculous. An amazing openness comes over us the more we relax this area. Try it.

Suddenly your face feels smooth and placid and the tension just pours off. We start to understand that we may have areas of tension of which we are unaware. We begin to see that our habits, those things we do unconsciously to make us feel comfortable, might be in our way. We need to examine more closely how we hold our body in everyday life. We need to discover the areas of unconscious tension and remind ourselves to relax those places. In this work, habit is our enemy.

The third area that Strasberg wants us to work on are the muscles "...leading along the side of the nose...that lead into the mouth and chin."[3] You see it all the time. People, usually when unobserved, work their mouths and lips in all kinds of unconscious motions. We too have developed odd ticks around our mouth. We realize, as we try to let these muscles relax, that when we are daydreaming or reading, we suck in part of our cheeks and chew lightly on the insides of them. What a disgusting revelation! We are carrying a tremendous amount of tension around in these muscles and people have probably noticed. We're going to work extra hard to relax this muscle group and to lose this horrible habit.

Other areas that hold tension are the neck, and the shoulders. We pay extra attention to these parts of our body, sending mental messages to them to let go. Sometimes an image is helpful. We imagine a warm heat flowing into the muscles of the neck and over our shoulders. We move our necks slowly and rotate our arms.

Finally, we feel completely relaxed. But when the instructor raises our arm and then lets go of it, it stays up, instead of dropping. Amazing. We are still holding tension in it.

The instructor offers us a strange solution to our problem. He asks us to drop our arm and then to tense it as hard as we can. We obviously look confused because the teacher immediately explains to us that relaxation can sometimes be achieved through its opposite. This seems a novel idea. We go ahead and tense our left arm. After a few moments of exertion, the instructor tells us to release our arm. He tells us to shake it out. We do. He asks us to tense and release it again. We do. He lifts the arm up, and when he lets it go, it flops back down. It worked. We remember that thinking in terms of opposites can be a very useful thing.

After the actor is relaxed, she may be asked to make sounds. These should surprise the actor and not be pre-planned. They often express whatever feelings have been aroused by the process of letting go. "…Things lying below the surface begin to come up and truly emotional things begin to happen, released by nothing more than relaxation."[4] If someone walked into a Method class at this point, they might think the people were crazy. Slouched in chairs and moaning, crying, laughing or screaming the actors might easily be mistaken for mental patients. In fact, this very thing has plagued the Actor's Studio for years. People did drop in and watch just single sessions of Method work and then ridicule it in print. Much of the prejudice against Strasberg's work originated from stories written by people with little or no exposure to the entire sequence of training.

Another misunderstanding concerning relaxation must also be cleared up at this point. Strasberg never advocated the removal of all tension from the actor during performance. It was self-evident to him that some degree of tension was necessary in the body to stand upright and to move. Strasberg wanted to remove *unnecessary* tension from the actor so that his energy could be free for the tasks demanded of him. The idea is to have as much tension in the body as is needed and no more. Strasberg wanted the actor to be dynamic on the stage, not sluggish or idle. Relaxation is not the goal of acting, only a starting point.

For Strasberg, all work begins at the relaxation level. But he knew, just as Stanislavski did, that relaxation is not enough. It must be complemented by its twin, concentration.

CONCENTRATION

Actors concentrate best when they are relaxed and relax best when they are concentrated. This was Stanislavski's basic idea and Strasberg subscribed to it absolutely. In Strasberg's work, the keys to concentration lie in the five senses.

After we have achieved a high level of relaxation, our teacher asks us to listen to the sounds in the room. When we do this, we notice the hum of the electric lights, the breathing of the other students, the movement of their clothes against their bodies, and the footfalls of our instructor. Next, he asks us to cast our hearing outside of the room and to listen only to those sounds. For the first time, we notice the sounds of traffic and the barking of dogs. We listen to the different sounds made by cars approaching and cars leaving, we think we hear a child's faint voice.

Now the instructor tells us that we are in a fixed orbit above the Earth. In our ship, he says, we posses a unique kind of volume control. With it, we can isolate any sound on the planet we want, and screen out all the others. He tells us to turn up the sound of all the laughter happening on the Earth right now. We imagine turning up this control. The teacher asks us if we are hearing a lot of laughter, or a little. He asks us if it is a mix of high and low voices, or of a single type.

Next, he us tells us to turn down the sounds of the laughter and to turn up the sounds of all the gunshots going off on the Earth at this very moment. We do. Is it a lot, he asks, or a little? Too many, we think to ourselves. Suddenly we hear the instructor telling us in a quiet voice to relax the muscles at the bridge of our nose. In concentrating on these sounds, we have put tension in our face. We do as he says. The teacher then asks us to turn down the gunshots, and to turn up the sounds of all the kissing going on all over the world. We cannot help but smile. This is a pretty good one.

After the exercise, the teacher makes the point that some of the sounds we listened to were real and actually going on, and that some were made real by the magic of our imaginations. He tells us that we are going to extend this exercise to our other senses.

The instructor puts before us a patterned plate. He asks us to observe it in detail for five minutes. We take the plate and examine it. After five interminable minutes, he takes it away. He then asks us to describe it. This, we think, will be easy, we've been staring at it for an eternity!

When we finish our description, the teacher asks us how heavy it is. Well, we say we really hadn't noticed. Were there any raised surfaces on the plate, he asks, or was the texture completely smooth all the way around? We confess we're not sure, we didn't feel all the parts of the pattern. When he shows us the plate again, we realize how inadequate our description of it was. We even got the order of the colored stripes wrong. We are amazed at our failure. It should have been so simple. The instructor reassures us. People must be trained to really observe, he says. The more we do it, the better we will be at it.

But he is not done with us. He hands the plate back to us and gives us one minute more with it. This time when he takes it away, he makes a strange request. He asks us to recreate the object. We stare. He tells us to close our eyes and create the plate with our imagination. We put our hands out as if we are holding the plate. We feel silly. We turn it over quickly, put our hand under it, fake eating off of it, and so on. But pretty soon the teacher stops us. He tells us that he is not looking for a pantomime, but a sensory recreation of the object. He asks us to let our fingers feel the coolness of the plate, to let our hands and arms feel the weight of it. After some moments, we can feel these things. He asks us to remember its color and shape, to see the patterns and how it reflects light. This imaginary plate is beginning to come to life for us. Not as a mimed object, but as a sensory experience. We feel a deep connection with this imaginary object and are newly respectful of the power of the imagination.

The teacher tells us that relaxation, concentration and imagination are all bound up together in this work. That when used jointly, they can help us to create imaginary objects for the audience. When we look out, say, at an imaginary cherry orchard, the audience will feel as though they too can sense its reality. This, he explains, is the essence of acting; creating things that aren't there. Creating imaginary relationships, behaving in imaginary circumstances, acting as if we were someone else, these are all acts of the imagination, which functions best when it is relaxed and concentrated.

The instructor now tells us that we are ready to move on to the next exercise. He asks us to go out and have a cup of coffee. We're beginning to like this guy. He wants us to remember all the sensations involved in having this coffee and recreate them in class.

SENSE MEMORY

A Cup of Coffee

When we do our exercise for the class, the teacher finds our work too general and superficial. He asks us questions. Do you feel the weight of the cup? Do your nails make a sound against the surface of the cup when you first grip it? What do your fingers feel like on the handle? Which fingers are in contact with the cup? Are your fingers hot? How hot? How full is the cup? Does the weight of the cup affect your wrist? What color is the coffee? Is there milk in it? Has it completely blended in yet, or can you see lighter and darker areas? What is the cup made of? Can you smell the aroma? What part of your lip comes in contact with the cup first? Is that first contact pleasant, or is the edge of the cup too hot? Does the smell change as the cup comes closer to your mouth? What is the first taste like? Is it bitter and then sweet, or the other way around?

Some of these questions we cannot answer. We simply don't remember. We want to go out right away and drink a cup of coffee. Is it bitter first, or sweet? The instructor asks us to do the exercise again tomorrow. When we come back the next day, we do better. We are beginning to understand just how much concentration this exercise requires.

Shaving or Makeup

The men in the class have been asked to shave, and the women to put on makeup at home. When we come back to class, we each do our best to recreate the sensory experience with imaginary objects. Some are more successful than others. This time, we get caught up in miming the actions of shaving, and don't really experience the sensory reality of the blade against our skin. The instructor has us do the exercise again. It takes us four times before we do it right. Sometimes it's like that.

Sunlight

The instructor has asked us to lie out in the sun and to note the feel of the sun's brightness and heat on our bodies. This one seems simple. But when we try it in class, we feel as if we are doing nothing. We sit in a chair with our heads tilted up, and our eyes closed. That's it. There is no activity to do. The teacher comments that we are just sitting there. It's true, we are. Relax the muscles of your face, he suggests. We didn't think they were tense, but when we do as he asks, we realize that they were. He guides us through the sensory reality of the sunshine, and we begin to recapture the feel of it. Others have trouble with this one too, so we don't feel quite so bad. We keep at it until we succeed in capturing that sunshine.

The Shower

Go home and take a shower, the teacher tells us next, but take it in a special way. Focus on the experience of your senses, he says. Note the temperature of the water, and the feel of its pressure. Note the smell of the enclosure, and the rising steam. See the size of the drops, the shower head, the handles, feel the reaction of your skin, note where the drops first hit. Remember the feel of the soap, it's weight, see its color, size and texture. Note how you use it. Do you put it under the water first to warm it up? Which part of your body do you soap up first? How does it feel on your skin? Does the water suddenly go cold when someone uses water elsewhere in the house? Notice when your eyes are open and when they are closed. Note the sound of the water as it hits your body, as it hits the floor, as it hits the shower curtain or glass. Let your body respond to the feeling of the water.

Pay attention to the sensory detail, because you are going to come in and recreate your shower for us, he says. But, he reiterates, DO NOT MIME IT! When you come in, the goal will be to awaken your memory of the sensory experience, not to show us how well you can recreate the soap.

When we bring in our "shower exercise", the teacher seems pleased. He tells us that we did successfully recreate the sensory experience of the shower. We feel pretty good. And cleaner.

We realize that in doing these sense memory exercises, our focus has mercifully gone off of ourselves and onto an imaginary reality. Our self-conscious energy has been redirected, and as a result, we have stopped watching ourselves. Thank goodness.

Personal Object

The instructor has now asked us to find an object at home for which we have a special feeling. This is the first time we have been assigned an exercise that specifically calls for an emotional reaction. He asks us to handle it and note all of its sensory reality, not to focus on the emotion it evokes. But not to avoid it either. If emotion comes, let it come, he says, but do not force it. Observe the object's color, size, smell, shape, sound, feel, texture, taste. We choose our deceased father's gold watch.

When we come into class the next day, we recreate the object. At first we simply see the imaginary watch, and then we pick it up. We feel the weight of it and notice that some of the golden color has rubbed off. We suddenly associate this loss of gold with the loss of our father, and we begin to sob. The sob becomes a torrent. When the instructor asks us to stay with the sensory reality of the object, we cannot do it. We are caught up in uncontrollable sorrow. This exercise has unlocked a deep well of feeling. The instructor gently guides us back to the object, asking us to describe it. Through gulps of air and with a painfully constricted throat, we do. When we finish, the teacher has a few words to say.

He tells us that when doing this work it is often best to use something seven years or older. This is because fresher memories are more difficult to control. He further explains that the Method is not only about expressing honest and deep emotion, but about controlling that expression. He says that what happened to me, while valuable and true, was something that we want to avoid. That is, emotion that we cannot control. He asks me when I received this object. We tell him that our father died ten months ago, and that we got the watch at that time. The lesson is clear. We need to use something much older. Some emotional distance is required.

This has been an important session. We were under the impression that Method work was all about the display of feeling. Even to the point of indulgence. What the instructor is now making clear however, is that a higher value is placed on truthful emotional expression that is repeatable and controllable. We begin to understand that this is what Strasberg means by an inner technique; something you can do over and over again.

Over the course of many weeks, we do many more sense memory exercises. These are usually combinations of other exercises. For instance, using a personal object in a particular room, or recreating a particular sensation such as sunshine with a personal object. The combinations are challenging. We feel our recall of sense memories improving significantly.

The Private Moment

The instructor says we are now ready to move on. He introduces us to the private moment exercise. He tells us that Lee Strasberg created this exercise as an extension of Stanislavski's idea of "public solitude." Remember, that Stanislavski felt it necessary for actors to feel private in public. In order to achieve this, he created exercises in the "circle of concentration," and with "objects of attention" (see pages 32-34). Strasberg wanted to take this a step further. He felt that the private moment would engage the actor's sense of concentration so fully that all thoughts of the audience would disappear. The private moment could give the actor an unparalleled experience of public solitude.

The private moment involves doing something that other people do not see you do, or that if they did, you would change the moment you noticed they were there.

The teacher tells us to recreate in the class, the room at home in which the private moment takes place. That means we can bring in all kinds of objects from home and put them in the playing space.

We feel a bit suspicious of this exercise because we've heard stories about it. This is one of those famous Actor's Studio activities that some people consider indulgent. The very thought of doing something personally private in public, makes us extremely anxious. We try to calm ourselves down. After all, maybe in overcoming our fear of this exercise, we will have a "breakthrough," one of those moments when we will arrive at a new and higher level of work.

But what private moment should we do? We know that some have put on music and danced with great abandon just as they sometimes do in the privacy of their own room. We know that others have done something so simple as to prepare for a night's sleep. What, we ask ourselves, do we do that we would immediately change if someone saw us? Suddenly we know.

In class the next day, we bring in the mirror from our bedroom and place it on a desk. We also put our toothbrush, toothpaste and electric shaver out. We begin by walking up to the mirror and looking at our reflection. We put toothpaste on the brush, but do not use it. We pick up the shaver, but put it back down again. Quit stalling, we tell ourselves, and do the exercise.

We stare into the mirror again. Finally, we come to the moment of truth, and slowly, we remove our shirt. As we stand before the all-seeing mirror, we let our stomach relax and check how far it sticks out. If someone were to walk in at this very moment, we would suck it back in.

After a few moments of appraisal, we sling our shirt back over our body. Before we turn back to the class, we take a deep breath. This has been extremely difficult for us to do. We stared into the mirror for many minutes before we could take off our shirt. We always try to present a fairly "fit" image to the world, even though we know we are not in the greatest shape. Even at the beach we do not take our shirt off because we do not like the way we look. We turn to the instructor.

He tells us that the exercise had all of the elements of a true private moment and yet did not succeed. We are stunned. Not succeed? We revealed something in public that we would never let anyone see, we protest.

Perhaps, he says gently, that is the problem. You did the exercise as though you knew that an audience was present. In the real moment at your mirror at home, you do not have to summon up the courage to look at your waistline like you did here, do you? Don't you just do it because you know no one is going to see you? You acted as though you were doing a very brave thing in front of a bunch of people. Which, no doubt you were, but the awareness of the public was much too present in your exercise. Try again tomorrow, he tells us.

We are truly disappointed. Not only did we do something personally difficult, but we have to do it again tomorrow. We must admit, however, that the teacher has a point. We wouldn't have picked up the toothbrush and the shaver and just set them down again. We did that because we were distracted by the audience. We were not really concentrating on where we were, or on what we were doing. Tomorrow will be different, we promise ourselves.

Today, we take much more time feeling comfortable in the space. The objects we bring help us to sensorially recall our bedroom at home, and we do not approach the mirror until we have established a strong "where." This time, when we take off our shirt, we really look at ourselves. And although we are not overjoyed at what we see, neither is it as horrible as we thought yesterday. In fact, we might be losing a little weight.

We look at the "spare tire" around our waist that we hate so much, and unconsciously check how many inches of flesh it is with a pinch of our fingers. We are amazed to find that it has shrunk since the last time we checked. Suddenly, and for no reason at all, we suck in our stomach, flex our muscles, and strike a ridiculous body builder pose. With a stupid grin on our face, we put our shirt back on and walk away from the mirror.

The instructor is smiling. He tells us that this private moment achieved what the other did not; a real sense of privacy and a true loss of audience awareness. He liked the moments of uninhibited behavior, he says, like the pinching and the posing. The posing, he points out, could have been a trap, in that it might have been done as a kind of "wink" to the audience, but that instead, it came across as something playful that we did for ourselves. We did not fall into the trap of "performing" our private moment, he says, but really achieved privacy in public. We are quite pleased and pleasantly surprised. We expected this exercise to be agony. And it was when we did it incorrectly the first time. But this time, it actually felt liberating. We do wonder though whether this exercise would actually help us onstage during a performance.

In fact, we are beginning to realize that all of the exercises we have done so far we have done by ourselves, and without a written text. We have done no scenes and have not yet worked with a scene partner. The instructor explains that first we work on ourselves, and then on a role. This, he tells us, is how both Stanislavski and Strasberg proceed. We have, he explains further, been using improvisational situations all along. Wasn't our private moment a "scene," he asks. We acknowledge that it was. Don't worry, he assures us, we'll get to scenes soon enough. First, he tells us, we must work on ourselves; on our relaxation, concentration, imagination and sense memory. Perhaps we are being a little impatient.

Animals

At the old American Lab, Maria Ouspenskaya used an exercise based on the observation of animals to break actors of habitual movement patterns and as the basis for physical characterizations. Our teacher tells us that Lee Strasberg found these exercises of great use and that we too would now do them.

He tells us to visit the zoo or to watch our animals at home. He tells us to observe carefully how the animal moves, where the center of gravity is, how the animal uses each part of its body, how the animal relates to its surroundings, what kinds of sounds the animal makes and when it makes them. He asks us to observe how the animal sleeps, and how it eats.

See what catches the animal's attention, he says, try to think like the animal and understand why it does what it does. After a considerable amount of observation, the instructor tells us to try and become the animal. Then we are to evolve the animal to human form while retaining some of the animal's features. We are to practice this at home and then do it in class. He tells us that Lee J. Cobb used the image of an elephant as the basis for his characterization of Willy Loman in Arthur Miller's *Death of a Salesman.*[5] The actor and teacher Allan Miller used the image of a cockroach to capture a character's "manic physical alertness,"[6] our instructor explains further. Using animals can propel us toward new ways of using our bodies and aid us in finding tempo-rhythms that differ from our own.

We spend part of the next day observing our friend's new puppy. The sheer energy impresses and exhausts us. We work hard and are happy with the results.

When we bring it in the next day for our exercise, we are able to actually think the puppy's thoughts. So that when we bring it up to human form, and the teacher tells us that we are in a bar, we immediately become an exuberant waiter eager to please each and every customer.

The teacher then changes the activity to a household chore. He asks us to vacuum the rug as this human with puppy characteristics would. We do. He is pleased. He then asks us to combine our private moment with this puppy/human. This gives us pause. The private moment we did, we did as ourselves, not as some character. He tells us to just do it. We try, but fail. We cannot achieve the same sense of privacy or of inner feeling that we had originally. He tells us to try it again tomorrow.

Today, we were able to transform the puppy's eager energy into a nervous anxiety that we could integrate into our private moment. The teacher expresses satisfaction with what we have achieved, and issues a new challenge.

He asks us to mix, with our puppy/human and our private moment, a sensation. Instantly, we choose a cold early morning and add it in. All of our senses are working now, and we find that the cold helps us with the nervous energy of the puppy. As we assess ourselves in the mirror, we rub our stomach in order to generate some warmth. The reality of the room has increased by sensorially creating a temperature, and when the exercise is over, we begin to see how valuable it can be to mix elements in our work. Sensations, private moments, personal objects, and animals all add substance to our presence on stage. The instructor is sufficiently pleased with our progress that he assigns us an exercise in emotion memory.

Affective Memory

Much has been said and written about affective memory. The first point to clear up about it, says our teacher, is that the actor does not simply recall a feeling. Going back in one's mind in order to find a past emotion to drag up, is not using affective memory. Emotion is usually quite resistant to a direct assault of this type. The instructor tells us: "The basic idea of affective memory is not emotional recall but that the actor's emotion on the stage should never be really real. It always should be only remembered emotion. An emotion that happens right now spontaneously is out of control…Remembered emotion is something that the actor can create and repeat; without that the thing is hectic."[7]

We are surprised by this. We always thought that real emotion happening spontaneously was what the Method was all about. This idea is different from Stanislavski's, it seems. He believed that if you enter the given circumstances of the play with belief and imagination and follow the actions of the part in concert with the super-objective, emotion would flow. And yet, in his first book, *An Actor Prepares,* he wrote much about affective memory. And herein lies part of the confusion.

The three books on acting technique that Constantine Stanislavski wrote during the course of his lifetime had a very peculiar publishing history. The first, *An Actor Prepares,* focused on the actor's inner technique, while the second, *Building A Character,* focused on the actor's external technique. Originally, these two volumes were meant to be published together. But this did not happen. *An Actor Prepares* was published in 1936, but *Building A Character* was not available in

English until 1949! And the third book, *Creating A Role* was not published in English until 1961. This last book contains Stanislavski's ideas from the 1930's which he called the *Method of Psycho-Physical Actions.* So, due to this unfortunate publishing history, Lee Strasberg and others were somewhat misled into emphasizing internal techniques over external ones.

When Strasberg discovered, from Stella Adler's report on her work with Stanislavski, that the Russian master no longer found affective memory useful, he felt betrayed. His successes as a director and teacher at the Group Theater were based on such exercises. So he stayed with them. In fact, for Strasberg, affective memory is the core of an actor's inner technique.

So, if affective memory is not the experiencing of spontaneous emotion, what is it, and how is it done? Affective memory, our instructor says, is based on conditioning. Remember Ivan Pavlov? our teacher asks. He was the Russian biologist who conditioned dogs to salivate at the sound of a bell even though no food was present. In the same way, emotions can be aroused if certain factors are put into play, he says. Stanislavski realized that by recreating the sense memories of an emotional event, the emotion itself would appear. The real memory involved then is sensory, not emotional. The actor does not focus on the feeling, but on the physical circumstances surrounding the emotional event.

The instructor asks us to remember a significant emotional moment in our lives that occurred at least seven years ago. More recent memories are usually less controllable, he says.

He asks us to relax into our chairs and then to recreate all the sensory details we can around the chosen event. He tells us to remember the place, what we wore, the temperature, what we smelled, what we heard, and what we said. He asks us questions that sharpen the details of our recollections. If we are in a room, what colors are the walls? How high do they reach? Of what material are they made? If we ran our fingers across the walls, what would they feel like? He asks us to remember how our clothes felt against our bodies, what they looked and smelled like, and if they were tight or loose. He asks us to remember in detail the smells of the place and of the people.

He asks us to remember the quality of the light in the room, and to recall the sounds and voices we heard.

All of these physical details bring the moment we are using to vivid life, and yet we cannot recapture the emotions associated with it. The instructor tells us that that is fine. He explains that sometimes one must try several memories before one works. The important thing is not to force the emotions.

After a few weeks, we hit upon a memory that stimulates a strong emotional reaction. We have been doing the exercise at home and in class for some time now, and we are elated to have found some success. It took us over an hour before the feelings began to flow, but flow they did. The teacher is encouraged by our success and tells us to do it again.

The next time we try, it takes forty-five minutes to arrive at the emotion. The next few times we use this memory, it takes us only half an hour to achieve success. We are indeed conditioning a response. After some more time, we are able to arrive at the emotion in only a few minutes. We no longer need to take so much time to relax and we do not need to mentally note and experience every individual sense memory. The teacher tells us that we now have one golden key that will open the door to our emotions. He tells us that we must continue to find more such memories so that we can have many golden keys. Maria Ouspenskaya told her pupils that she had twelve of them.

How though, we wonder, do we use an affective memory in our work? As an exercise, it certainly opens up great wells of feeling, and even has given us a measure of control over those feelings, but how does it work in performance? This of course is the subject of great controversy.

We remember how some actors in the Group Theater complained that their scene partners would drop out of a moment in order to do an affective memory exercise for an upcoming emotional demand.

The instructor tries to quell our doubts by telling us how affective memories work in a scene. He says that the actor finds an affective memory that closely corresponds to the emotion demanded by the scene. He then practices the exercise until he is able to make it work in about a minute with the dialogue and action of the scene. So, the actor actually practices the exercise using the words of the scene. Not initially, of course. First, the actor needs to make sure the memory is one that works and is repeatable. After that has been achieved, the actor slowly adds in the words of the text.

There is no question that the use of emotion memory can be effective. Even Quintilian suggested remembering an event in life that could help the orator empathize with a current situation. He knew that this would make an orator's arguments more persuasive.

Stanislavski too realized the value of recalling events from the past and using them in the present. But later in his life he found that too great an emphasis on creating feeling led the actor astray. Years later, Robert Lewis put the problem this way, "You're on the stage and you've got this feeling. It somehow blinds you and deafens you so that you don't really see, you don't really hear, you don't really play the action of the moment, but you hang on because it is a marvelous feeling. The trick was to release yourself from the exercise as you came in and play whatever the situation was, so that the feeling that you had in you went up and down normally the way emotion does in life..."[8]

Another problem surfaced for the actors of the Group Theater. Some of them found that the affective memories no longer worked night after night. Strasberg felt that this failure had nothing to do with the technique itself, but with the actor's use of it. He felt that they must be doing the exercise incorrectly. And indeed, when he would guide them through the sensory details of the memory, he would discover that they had been leaving out important items. With proper guidance, the exercise would work again.

For Strasberg, the well-trained actor posseses conditioned emotional responses that can be turned on and off at will. It is, in fact, this ability that makes an actor an artist. And that is why so much importance and emphasis is placed on sense and affective memory exercises at the Actor's Studio.

What about dropping out of a scene in order to do an exercise? Well, it doesn't really matter if the moment being acted is a close-up in a film. Many actors have found that the greatest use of affective memory is before the cameras. For take after take, this exercise can be tremendously useful. When the camera is focused mostly, or exclusively on one actor, that actor needn't worry about the connection with his scene partner. In such a situation, it is the believability of the emotion that is paramount. And so it is here, that affective memory really comes into its own. It is perhaps for this reason that so many Actor's Studio trained actors are so successful on film.

But on the stage, the use of affective memory can clearly pose problems. Stanislavski thought he found a simpler way to arouse emotion, and stopped using it. But others swear by the power and effectiveness of affective memory, and they cannot be ignored. Some of America's finest actors have been trained at the Actor's Studio in this technique and find it useful.

The Song and Dance Exercise

The instructor has another exercise for us. He asks us to pick a simple song like "Mary Had a Little Lamb." He tells us to stand in front of the class and to stay completely still. Instead of singing the song in its usual rhythm, we are to make each of its notes nearly equal in length. We don't have to be faithful to the melody either.

When we try this, we find it hard to stay still. We also find it difficult to sever the song from its rhythm. But after many attempts, we succeed. The instructor then asks us to make a dramatic movement with our body during the song. He then asks us to make lots of movements during the course of the song, and not in the expected rhythmic places.

When we try this, we feel embarrassed. Leaping about and making sounds in this way makes us feel extremely silly. But the instructor explains that it is important for us to know that about ourselves.

Sometimes a part requires us to be silly, and we must be free enough to express it.

We try the exercise again and after a while, we do it with real abandon and a genuine sense of fun. When it is over, we share our feelings with the instructor and the class. We feel that most of our emotional expression in the class has been of a closed-in kind. But this exercise made us feel open and expansive. In the other exercises we were afraid of being too big, or of doing too much. But in this one, we say, our fear of large expression disappeared.

The instructor tells us that bigness is often required of the stage actor, and that the kind of energy we displayed in the song and dance exercise is what is needed. Too often, he says, actors think that Strasberg's work requires them to be small, or casual. This is nonsense, he tells us. It is phoniness that Strasberg objects to, not bigness. If the emotional underpinnings are genuine, any size performance can be justified.

❄

As we leave class, we realize that we have had a lot of preconceptions smashed. Strasberg, contrary to our long-standing prejudice, did not teach actors to be mumbling, emotionally erratic performers. If some became so under his guidance, it was more their failure than his. He tried, all of his teaching and directing life, to help actors become artists capable of expressing and controlling honest and powerful emotion. His "private moment" and "affective memory exercises" were and remain controversial. Their usefulness still a matter of debate. But actors and teachers trained by him continue to use them, nonetheless. Some Actor's Studio members went into psychotherapy during their training, and we cannot help but think of the fear that existed for 1,800 years that acting could harm an actor both physically and mentally. Perhaps, at some extreme level, the actor's exploration of himself can threaten his stability. And yet we are usually capable of pushing ourselves further than we think, so it is difficult to say.

Strasberg can certainly be criticized for paying less attention to actions, given circumstances, objectives and characterization than he might have. And his personal aloofness and legendary outbursts of fury must have intimidated and even inhibited many. But no one dedicated himself more fiercely to the actor's exploration of himself than did this master teacher.

Sitting in a chair at the Actor's Studio, with only his intellect and uncanny insight to guide him, Lee Strasberg helped to prove that actors can be artists. When he someday meets Gordon Craig, he can greet him with a smile.

Chapter 6
Stella Adler

Jacob and Sara Adler were two of the finest actors of the American Yiddish theater. They were a significant part of a vital ethnic theatrical scene that thrived in New York from the late nineteenth century well into the 1950's. Adler's daughter, Stella, was born in New York City in 1902, and was destined to become the most famous and influential member of the family. She began her acting career at the age of four and concluded it fifty-five years later, in 1961. During that time, and for years after, Stella Adler taught. With the full force of her formidable energy, she dedicated herself to transmitting to others, the craft that served her so well. Her pupils are some of the most illustrious performers in both theater and film; Marlon Brando chief among them.

When Stella Adler attended Boleslavsky's American Lab Theater in the late twenties, she was already an established actress with a high reputation. But she wanted more. The other members of the Adler acting family made fun of what they called her "seriousness." But she persevered despite the teasing. Although tempted by the glamour of Broadway, Adler was always more dedicated to artistic excellence, and that desire informed all of her creative choices in both teaching and acting.

Stella Adler was an original member of the Group Theater, but was ambivalent about it from the beginning. Along with Morris Carnovsky, she was the most experienced actor in the troupe, and she was often frustrated with the amateur antics of some of the other members. She was also uneasy with main Group director and acting teacher, Lee Strasberg. But despite her suspicion of some of Strasberg's methods, she continued with the Group throughout its turbulent but glorious history.

When she returned from her work with Stanislavski in Paris, she began teaching classes for the members of the Group. They often found themselves more stimulated by what she was teaching than by what they found with Strasberg. Adler had come back with a chart, and a personal working knowledge of Stanislavski's system, and this gave her words a special authority. She spent the rest of her life paying Stanislavski back for the help and insights he had given her.

In 1949, Adler opened her own acting studio. When she died in 1992, there were two Stella Adler Conservatories; one in New York, and one in Los Angeles. Both schools continue despite her passing.

Stella Adler's teachings are often contrasted with those of Lee Strasberg. This happens most obviously when the topic of affective memory is broached. It should be remembered that Adler had trouble with emotion memory work before she ever met Stanislavski. As an actress, she had very little problem with finding and communicating the proper emotion for a scene, and felt that delving into her personal life, as affective memory required, was unnecessarily invasive. But because she felt that affective memory was an essential part of the Stanislavski system, she reluctantly used it.

Working with Stanislavski however, relieved her of having to use emotional recall, and her joy in performing returned.

Like Stanislavski, Adler placed greatest emphasis on imagination, circumstances and actions. If an actor did enounter problems in summoning up an emotion, she would allow that actor to search for a parallel experience in his life, but only in order to retain the playable actions from that memory. What does this mean?

Suppose we are cast as a restaurant consultant. And suppose further, that this consultant is a know-it-all with a superior attitude. Now imagine that when we portray this character, we find ourselves unable to believably locate the appropriate emotional tone. When an actor finds himself in such a difficulty, he might go out and study a real restaurant consultant. And while this can be useful, and in some cases crucial, it may not help the actor find what he is looking for.

Instead, Adler might suggest remembering times in the actor's own life when he has been consulted about something. She might ask, what are you an expert in? Perhaps the actor will answer that he is a real authority on stereo systems.

How, Adler might ask, do you talk to people who ask for your advice about stereos? The actor might then become quite animated, talking with passion about his love of good sound. Now, Adler says, suppose that I have a very inferior system. And suppose that I ask you your honest opinion of it. How would you talk, how would you sound? The actor might then begin gesturing and speaking rapidly as he dissects the faults of her system. These physical characteristics may help him find the emotional tone that is appropriate to the character of the restaurant consultant. All that is needed next, is for the actor to exchange his own words and topic, for the words and topic of the scene.

The actor doing this does not focus on the emotion itself, but on the physical embodiment of it; the gestures, the voice, the animation, these will all lead him to the feeling. In this way, the actor can use memory, but avoid indulgence. What about repeatability? Well, Remember Delsarte's soldier (p.11)? The physical characteristics will bring back the feelings. But Adler does not rely on experiences from the actor's personal life in order to arouse emotion.

❄

In our class, the instructor tells us that like Delsarte, Stanislavski and Strasberg, Adler believes that "tension is one of the absolute enemies of acting."[1] She believes that an actor must possess complete muscular control. In order to achieve this, the actor must do relaxation exercises. But then the actor should move on to muscular challenges. What, we wonder is a muscular challenge?

The teacher asks us to imagine that our left ankle is sprained. She tells us that the injury occured two weeks previously and that the ankle is now wrapped, but tender. We imagine this. Next, the instructor asks us to do simple tasks with this muscular challenge. We choose to cook breakfast. In our exercise, we enter an imaginary kitchen area, open an imaginary refrigerator, assemble imaginary ingredients on an imaginary table and…

The instructor stops us. She tells us that we have chosen too complicated a task and that we are focusing far too much on miming the actions. Keep it simple, she tells us. We think for a moment. We decide to simply tie our shoe. We enter with a slight hobble, favoring the left ankle. We then sit down and gingerly lift our left foot over our right knee. With care, we lean forward and slowly tie the lace. We stop in mid-tie to relieve the strain on our ankle caused by flexing our foot. After a moment's relaxation, we continue until the task is completed.

The teacher tells us that we showed good muscle control. She explains that when we focus on one part of our body, the rest of the muscles usually relax. Another benefit of this exercise, she says, is that it makes good use of our imaginations. We must use some type of sense memory to create the sprained ankle, and then must act logically within the circumstances of the injury. Imagination, she tells us, is the greatest quality an actor can have. With it, anything is possible, without it, nothing is. "…every word, every action, must originate in the actor's imagination."[2]

According to Adler, our instructor explains, "the actor's job is to defictionalize the fiction."[3] What does this mean? It means that even though the character, the events and the place are fictional creations of the playwright, the actor must live within them as though they are real. Accomplishing this is an act of pure imagination, and it is consistent with Stanislavski's Magic If. (p.36).

Emotion should ideally come from the actor's commitment to the circumstances. If the actor can make the situations in which characters find themselves vivid and believable, then emotion should flow naturally. So a clear and deep understanding of the given circumstances is critical for the actor's expressive truthfulness.

The first approach to a circumstance is the "where." Everything that happens, happens somewhere. A place has a profound effect on our behavior. We act differently in a locker room than we do in a throne room. It is no coincidence that the creator of improvisational Theater Games, Viola Spolin, often told improvisers that when they ran dry of inspiriation the "where" would save them.

So often in improv, Spolin would point out, the players just stand around trying to think of clever things to say. Soon, the improvisors run dry, and the scene dies. "Use the 'WHERE,'" she would say. If a scene is set in an old attic, and the players are stuck, they should return to the action of the scene, looking for an old hat for instance, and new ideas will come. Dealing with the "where" is a first priority in improvisational work, just as it is for Stella Adler.

But a circumstance is composed of more than a "where." A circumstance has a "when," a "what," and a "who" as well. And each of these must be thoroughly explored and understood before the actor can truly live in the circumstances.

Circumstances are also constantly shifting. Suppose, our teacher says, you come over to your fiancée's apartment in order to celebrate your six-month engagement. The circumstances the actor would need to understand would stretch at least as far back as their first meeting.

More immediately, he would have to know where he was coming from in the moments before his arrival, and to where he is going. Suppose he was coming from a dirty construction site, and had to quickly change into a tuxedo. The actor might then leave a smudge on his face or hands. The circumstance would determine this.

Suppose the relationship with his intended bride has been a smooth and untroubled one. Suppose further, that in his excitement to see her, he has decided to surprise her and come early. When he knocks on her door, he is feeling happy and playful. When there is no answer, he knocks again. Still, no answer. His feelings begin to alter, as the circumstance itself changes. She is not responding, and this concerns him. Mildly. There are degrees of shift in both emotion and circumstance.

He tries the door, and finds it yielding. He steps in and calls her name. No answer. He frowns in response to the circumstance, which is changing its nature. He begins methodically looking around the apartment to see if she's there. She is not. It takes a moment for the reality of this circumstance to hit him. Did he get the date wrong? The time? Did he forget something?

Then he sees her open closet door in the bedroom. It looks peculiar but he's not sure why. He crosses to it with increasing speed realizing on the way that there are no clothes in her closet. He instinctively turns, opens her drawers. They too are empty. This is an entirely new and dangerous circumstance. She's gone. Moved out? He stands stunned. He looks on her nightstand for a note, or some telltale phone message. There is nothing, no explanation. Why, he wonders? Where did she go? Is this a joke? Has she been kidnapped? This new circumstance elicits new thoughts and feelings. And these, in turn, elicit new actions. He picks up the phone and calls his fiancée's best friend. He is in a rising panic. What is going on?

If the actor playing this scene begins with clear circumstances and is committed to them, and is open to the shifts in those circumstances, the whole action of the scene will be believable and the emotions will be truthful. Of course, the more rich and detailed the actor's response to the changing circumstances, the deeper the scene will be.

You notice we spoke of actions just now. What are they? How did Adler understand and use them?

Simply put, "an action is something you do."[4] In the scene above, the man knocks on the door. That is an action. How he knocks on the door is a function of the circumstance. If he knew she was resting, he would knock on the door softly. If he needed to alert her to a fire in the building, he would pound on the door. Actions occur within circumstances. This is something Stanislavski stressed to Adler in Paris, and a point she insisted on in her own teaching.

Our teacher explains that Adler broke actions down into component parts called "activities." For example, if a character's action is to fly an airplane, she must engage in many smaller actions. She must check the fuel, get clearance from ground control, check the engines and pressure gauges, assess the weather and so on. These activities are in support of the larger action of flying the plane.

But why is the character flying the plane? The answer to this question, Adler calls the *justification.* In the pilot's case, the justification might be to save the life of a wounded man.

We must also understand, explains our teacher that Adler does not use Stanislavski's term "through-line-of-action," but her own phrase, *overall action.* For example, the overall action for the pilot might be to help win the war. So, for Adler, the *activities* and the *actions* must be *justified* and in support of the *overall action.* This is the same mix of the ideas of Stanislavski and Vakhtangov that the Group Theater used without the emphasis on *affective memory.*

So far we see that performing logical actions in imaginative circumstances is of great importance in Stella Adler's work and teachings. Her focus is squarely on the author's text. Not just the words of it, but on the whole complex webbing of character and circumstance. It is no wonder that for years, she toured the country teaching classes in script analysis. She did not believe in wandering far from the world of the play itself. Her goal was to unite the actor and his part within the boundaries of the text.

While Lee Strasberg spent a great deal of time opening up the actor's emotional life, Stella Adler focused on the actor's creation of character.

Our instructor tells us that we must do vocal and physical work in order to have the necessary energy to perform a character on the stage. This readiness is essential, she tells us, if we are to transform our daily selves, into living characters.

The first step toward characterization, she explains, is a thorough understanding of the circumstances of the play. Next, we must narrow down our focus to the circumstances of our character. What is the educational level of our character? What financial background does the character come from, and what financial condition is he now in? What does the character do for a living, and what hobbies does he have? What is his relationship with his father, mother, brothers, sisters, wife, children, lover, boss, co-workers, pets? Today? In the past? The answers to these questions should yield playable results. It is not useful to create a character biography that cannot be used.

Suppose in our earlier scene, that the actor playing the man coming to see his fiancée decided that the character had seen a piano fall from a twelfth story window before arriving at her apartment. Now while this *preceding incident* is imaginative, it adds nothing to the scene to come. It is a detail that is irrelevant. A good character background is one that illuminates the subsequent behavior of the character. It cannot simply be a flight of fancy.

Our instructor tells us that tempo-rhythms play a strong part in Adler's approach to characterization as does the observation of animals.

If, for example, a character is easily distracted and has weak powers of concentration, the actor might choose to observe the behavior of a puppy. By doing this deeply, the actor begins to realize that the reason why the puppy turns its head toward everything new, is that he is always expecting something wonderful to happen. This attitude can then be transferred to human behavior.

Once believable behavior is mastered, the actor should put the character in circumstances both within and without the scene. Imagine this easily distracted character watching a movie, writing a story, disciplining a child, driving, waiting in a doctor's office, working out, cooking breakfast. Once behavior is found, the voice of the character may fall into place, or the voice may come first. The trick here is not to let characteristics become the character. If one only characterizes vocally, and the rest of the body and mind are not fully involved, the character will run the risk of being a caricature. And if one only plays a conglomeration of characteristics, a fully developed character will not emerge.

Most young actors, our teacher says, play characters like old men, or country bumpkins as clichés; as nothing more than a funny voice or a peculiar walk. They focus only on the external. An actor needs to develop a *sense of truth,* she explains. Without it, he cannot detect this falseness in himself.

Ask an actor to play a "nervous" character. Most likely they will wring their hands and look around a lot. But Adler would ask us to explore "nervousness" more deeply.

Let's pick a playable action that our nervous character might do in private, something to avoid embarrassment. Let's decide on nail biting. Now what we must next do is find some logical behavior that nail biting could cause. First of all it is a disgusting habit. At least let's suppose that this character thinks so. What behavior would be logical for this character to display in public regarding her hands? She would be embarrassed by their appearance, would she not? What playable action would result from this embarrassment? She would want to hide the tips of her fingers. See what happens if you try this.

The instructor sets up a living room space and creates a scenario for a male and female student. The scenario is this: The girl is having a date over for dinner. Before the meal, they sit in the living room and engage in some small talk.

When the actress sits, she folds her hands over one another in such a way that the tips of her badly bitten fingers cannot be seen. As the scene progresses, she offers her date a tray of snacks, but does it in a way that conceals her ragged nails. But most revealingly, when she leans over the table to retrieve the tray, the hand that supports her weight is curved inward, hiding her nails, but giving her the stance of an ape. Seeing this, her date cannot help but look at her hand. Her attempt to hide her nails has only focused attention on them. Her behavior has caused what she has been trying to prevent. For a terrible moment she catches his eye, mortified. Then she quickly moves her hand and sits back down.

The instructor is happy. You see, she says, by carrying out the logic of a nervous action, a real piece of original behavior was created. And when this logic results in playable actions, she continues, it is of tremendous use to an actor.

Now be clear, she says. In this exercise the covering of the hands did not create the nervousness, it helped to relieve it. As long as the character felt that her weakness was hidden, she could freely interact. But the minute her secret was even partly revealed, she lost her balance and self-confidence. It was in that moment that we saw more deeply into the character's inner life, and understood her vulnerability.

Following out the logic of a character element,[5] a circumstance, an action, a justification, this is the actor's job. It takes a clear mind, and a fertile imagination, she tells us.

This has been an important lesson. We have rarely seen a physical character choice carried out so logically and playably. We must learn to make this a solid part of our acting technique.

Now what about dialogue, the teacher asks. Aren't you curious about how to approach it? We haven't touched on it yet, you know. Suddenly everyone's attention is riveted to the front. Knowing that she has us, she slowly walks around the room saying nothing. Our attention is only heightened by this. She arrives at the blackboard and picks up a piece of chalk. Everyone scurries for a pencil and paper. But then she puts down the chalk, turns, and faces us. Eveyone stops. Her eyes wander off as if in thought. We are silent for fear of disturbing her. Her eyes return to us and a huge smile crosses her face. She bursts out laughing. We laugh too, knowing we've been caught in some snare.

We just played a scene together did we not, she asks. Yes, we all agree. What was the dialogue of this scene, she wants to know? There wasn't any, we say. But doesn't every scene begin and end with dialogue, she asks? We are silent. When you first look at your part in a scene or a play, don't your eyes first fall on the words you say? No one answers, but we all know it's true.

A play, she explains quietly, is a circumstance. A circumstance that contains within it places, things and characters. And these characters speak; sometimes to themselves, sometimes to each other. But in every case, the words they say only have meaning within a circumstance.

As an actor, always tell yourself, in your own words, the circumstances of the scenes you are in. The more you work on a role, the more circumstances you will come to understand. Find actions that are logical to the play's and the character's circumstances, and then paraphrase the dialogue your character says.[6] This will put the author's text in your own words. In this way you will be able to check yourself. You see, whatever you put in your own words will be what you understand, what has made an impression. When you look again at what the author wrote, you may discover that you have left out much of value. And whatever has been left out, has not been understood. Paraphrase again when you do understand all the important points that the author is making. Then the ideas and thoughts will belong to you.[7]

Play the truth and logic of the circumstances, live and do things imaginatively within them, and the dialogue will flow.

Stella Adler focused on imagination, circumstances, actions, justification and character just as Stanislavski did, our teacher says. And like him late in his life, she rejected affective memory as ultimately more destructive than helpful.

She brought the knowledge of a great working actress to her teaching which lent a great practicality to her approach. But remember this, our instructor cautions. All of her ideas, her Stanislavski-based approach, is only meant to be a help. It does not give you talent, nor does it guarantee success. If it does not work for you, try something else. But, our teacher concludes, I would be very much surprised if the techniques we have learned here do not come to your aid for the rest of your performing life.

Chapter 7

Sanford Meisner

Sanford Meisner was born in 1905 in Brooklyn, New York. He began his stage career as an extra with the Theater Guild after an education in music at the Damrosch Institute of Music. While at the Theater Guild, he studied acting, but found the instruction disappointing. Like Delsarte and Stanislavski before him, the standard route to training failed him.

It was when he met Harold Clurman and Lee Strasberg that his eyes were opened to what great acting and great theater could achieve. In 1931 he became an original member of their Group Theater. And as an actor there he achieved great success particularly in Odets' plays *Paradise Lost,* and *Awake and Sing:* "Sandy Meisner seized some of Odets' funniest, most characteristic dialogue ('I'm so nervous—look, two times I weighed myself on the subway station') and created an entire life behind it..."[1]

But like Stella Adler and Robert Lewis, Meisner had trouble with director and teacher Lee Strasberg's use of affective memory. He was also looking for ways to go beyond casual realism, and to find a way to use Stanislavski 's and Vakhtangov's work to create more stylized characters.

In the mid-1930's he began teaching, having been inspired by Strasberg, Adler, Michael Chekhov and by "...the lucid and objective approach of Sudakov and Rappaport."[2] These last two being Russian theorists and teachers. His tenure at the Neighborhood Playhouse in New York is legendary, as much for the quality of his teaching as for the many successful students who benefitted from it.

❄

At the Group Theater, Meisner was disturbed by the extensive use of paraphrasing. He felt that paraphrasing the plot, the circumstances and the dialogue of a play put the actor too much in his head. For Meisner, acting comes from the heart, not from the intellect. In this respect he differs greatly from Stella Adler, for whom paraphrasing is a valuable tool.

Another problem that bothered Meisner at The Group was the actor's loss of connection with his or her scene partner in order to do an affective memory exercise. Whether this was a failure of the method itself, or of the actor using it, is moot. It happened. And it greatly disturbed many of the actors. Meisner felt that the connection between actors was vital to the life of a scene, and that when that bond was broken, the acting lost its special quality and power. So in his teaching he focused on one of the most ignored elements of Stanislavski's system: *Communion* (p.53).

For Stanislavski, communion meant not only the communication between scene partners, but between the actor and himself, and between the actor and the audience. But Meisner was most interested in it as it related to scene partners.

Meisner realized that two actors could be in a scene, have created great characters, be playing proper actions, be emotionally truthful, and still fail the scene. What gave crackling energy and tension to a scene, he knew, was the interaction between the characters. The audience may enjoy a bravura solo performance, but they respond much more to the give and take of two, three or four characters fully engaged with one another.

This was the stuff of which great theater was made, and this was what most fully illuminated the fathomless complexity of the human soul; the dynamics between people, the body language, the tone of voice, the quality of the exchange between one human and another. "All of my exercises were designed to strengthen the guiding principle…that art expresses human experience,"[3] he has said.

Meisner has been bold enough to set out a definition of acting. It is this: "…living truthfully under imaginary circumstances."[4] The question then becomes, how does an actor accomplish this task? In the end, he felt that Strasberg's Actor Studio method was not the way. As much as he learned from Strasberg, Meisner one day told him, "You introvert the already introverted. All actors, I said, like all artists are introverted because they live on what's going on in their instincts, and to attempt to make that conscious is to confuse the actor."[5] No, he felt, another way must be found.

❄

In our first class, the teacher asks us to look at each other. We laugh in an embarrassed way as we look at the other students in the room. Really look, the instructor demands. So we really look. But the teacher stops and asks us if we are looking and seeing, or just trying to look like we are looking. We confess that we are sort of fake looking. Well, says the teacher, don't. Don't look because I told you to, look to see what's there.

Look to really see her shoes. Ask yourself what quality of the shoes stands out. Is it the color, the material, the shape? Look at his hair. What do you notice? Don't be afraid of the obvious. It's a Mohawk, isn't it? He has a Mohawk. Now look at me. Does anything catch your attention? If it does, say to yourself what it is, then move on to someone else. Go ahead, I'll wait, he tells us. Minutes go by as we all silently do this.

Good, the instructor says, you are really doing what you are doing. This is the essential element of the Meisner approach, he says. Meisner himself calls it the *reality of doing*.

Now look around the room again, and realize that every person in this room is your lifeline. Your work will depend on theirs. Just as mountain climbers are roped together because their safety depends on it, so your scenes will live or die depending on the invisible rope connecting you together. That rope may stretch thinner, it may grow stronger, it may even become frayed, but it must never break.

THE WORD REPETITION GAME

The instructor now asks us to make an observation about someone in the room. We spy the girl's shoes and say out loud "her shoes are red." But say it to her, the teacher says. We turn to her and say "your shoes are red." Next the teacher asks the girl with the red shoes to repeat back what we just said to her. She gives the instructor a stare, but says, "your shoes are red." Keep going, the teacher instructs us. Finally after seven or so repetitions he stops us. Excellent, says the teacher, and rubs his hands together. He seems happy, but the reason for this eludes us. What did we do that was good, we ask? Because as far as we're concerned we didn't do anything. The actress admits that she too is confused. All we did was say "your shoes are red" over and over again.

This exercise, which the teacher tells us is called the word repetition game, is a very important one. For one thing, the teacher explains, it makes us listen to each other. And for another, it places our focus outside of ourselves and onto the other person. In this way, self-consciousness has little time to develop.

Everyone in the class does this exercise, and one very similar to it wherein the participants respond in the first person. So instead of repeating "your shoes are red," the actress now says "my shoes are red." And with this change, comes a remarkable development. Emotion has made an appearance. Sometimes, during the exercise, laughter bubbles up. Sometimes tears. Often anger and sarcasm. This simple exercise is unleashing all kinds of unexpected energy.

After we do one that resulted in hysterical laughter, The instructor asks us "By the way, do you have an idea as to where your response came from? If you said the other person you are correct!"[6]

Sometimes we find ourselves trying to impress the class with a particularly outrageous way of doing this exercise, but the teacher corrects us. He asks us not to be interesting but to just stay with whatever is happening. He also tells us not to "try" so hard. He says, "trying to do the exercise right is not doing the exercise right. It is the TRYING that creates a tension that will shut down your availability."[7]

Next, the instructor extends the repetition exercise. He tells us to ask a question of our partner. One that is personal. And then to do the repetition with that question. He tells us that at some point, our instincts will tell us that we can change the words. This change, he explains, should come from a change in the behavior of our partner.

If we repeat "do you get nervous at auditions" five or six times, we may see a change take place in our partner. When we sense this change, we can change the words of the exercise to acknowledge this. We can now say, "this question upsets you." The partner will then repeat, "this question upsets me." After a time a change will again be sensed and the words can change to reflect it. The partner may then say "you're feeling guilty," and the one who first asked the question can say "I'm feeling guilty." It becomes clear to us that this exercise could go on for quite some time. It is rich.

After we do this extension of the word repetition game, the instructor asks us how we feel. We tell him that many honest and intense emotions passed between us. He tells us that we indeed did well, and that we truthfully played the reality in front of us. We did not force any emotions, but instead gave full value to the feelings that were aroused and did so without pushing.

Our initial skepticism about this whole repetition business is disappearing. We are beginning to see that working off a partner's response, determines our own; that the two of us are in an action-reaction dance that creates a palpable flow of energy between us. When we watch others engaged truthfully in this dance, it is compelling. We sometimes find ourselves on the edge of our seats waiting to see what will happen next.

THE KNOCK ON THE DOOR

The instructor tells us that we are now ready to move forward. So far, the teacher explains, we have been dealing with the "living truthfully" part of Sanford Meisner's definition of acting. Now we must add the "in imaginary circumstances" part.[8]

This exercise will again involve two of you, explains the teacher. One of you will be in a room doing something that is very difficult. This is crucial. It must be a real challenge to you. Do your taxes, for instance. It takes considerable concentration and the consequences for not getting them done are substantial. It must be something that engages your full attention. Your partner will then knock on the door and begin the repetition with you. The one in the room initially, must continue doing what they are doing and continue the repetition as well. And remember this critical phrase, "…don't do anything until something happens to make you do it."[9] Let's give it a try.

We decide on a task and a reason for doing it. The task is to glue seamlessly together the pieces of an antique vase that we broke. We need to do it so well that our parents will never suspect that it has been damaged. We bring in the actual pieces, since this is a true, ongoing event, and some glue. The teacher tells us to begin. We are not very good with our hands and find gluing the pieces together extemely difficult. We have to start over and over because the glue keeps leaking out the sides, and because we have trouble precisely lining up the pieces.

After our partner sees that we are absorbed in our problem, she knocks on the door, and comes into the room. We look up for a moment but instantly return to our task. She asks, "What's up?" We repeat, in a sarcastic tone, "What's up?" We are annoyed at the intrusion and the fact that she does not notice the obvious, that we are deeply involved in something else. She says again "What's up?" We sense a change and go with it. "I'm tied up right now," we say. "You're tied up right now," she replies, "I'm tied up right now," we repeat, getting exasperated. "You're tied up right now," she says again. "I'M TIED UP RIGHT NOW," we scream.

We have dropped and broken another piece of the vase. A few moments go by as she walks over to the scene of the disaster. "You're clumsy," she says. "I'm clumsy," we repeat as we pick up the broken pieces. She says more slowly, "You're clumsy." We sit back down dejectedly and repeat, "I'm clumsy." A few moments pass, and the teacher ends the exercise.

It isn't about the words is it, he asks? It's about "responding truthfully to the other person,"[10] right? We both agree. In this exercise, you must respond to the other person within the circumstance. The two of you created a scene that had strong emotions running through it, but little dialogue. No great speeches or monologues, just a situation, and each other. And for a few moments you created something compelling.

Now let me ask you a question. Were you, asks the instructor, aware of us out here? No, we reply, neither of us were. So your concentration on the task and on each other was enough to remove the distraction of an audience? Yes, we reply, it was. We realize, with some delight, that we had attained Stanislavski's state of "public solitude" (p 34). Cool.

This technique is definitely helping us to establish a living relationship with our fellow players. It dawns on us that we have never worked by ourselves in this class, but only with a partner. So many of Strasberg's and even Adler's exercises were done alone, by ourselves. Meisner's committment to Stanislavski's idea of communion is certainly strong.

Another benefit, we realize, is that we are present in each moment. Because we are not certain how our partner is going to respond, we musy really listen, and in order to do that, we must be alive in every moment. We have heard of "moment-to-moment" acting, but now we have experienced it. It is critical to this work.

But what about applying all of this to scenes, we wonder. It's all right going moment-to-moment, but what if the moment doesn't fit the scene? How do we structure a part if we are simply playing the reality of each moment? And where does Meisner stand on the question of emotion? We know he rejects affective memory, but what does he accept?

The instructor seems to read our minds. He tells us that when it comes to scenes, Meisner wants actors to learn their lines by rote, with no "line readings" or interpretation. Meisner wants the lines learned mechanically. This is done to keep the actor from learning preconceived ways of saying the lines. Lines are usually learned away from one's partner, and actors are therefore deprived of the stimulus that will truthfully animate the dialogue. To avoid this, the actors learn their lines without meaningful inflections. But, the instructor tells us, we'll learn more about scene work another time. For the moment he wants to address the problem of emotion.

Meisner was very much impressed and influenced by the great actor, Michael Chekhov, our teacher reminds us. And you will of course remember that Chekhov felt strongly that emotions could be aroused by the imagination (p.63). In Meisner's work, the imagination too plays a strong role in the generation of feeling. But for Meisner, this excitation of feeling should only occur offstage before an entrance. Once on stage, the circumstances and other players should be fuel enough for the continuance and natural change of the actor's feelings.

In the offstage moments, our teacher suggests that we use either the given circumstances of the the play to arouse feeling, or use Vakhtangov's adjustment (p.61). You of course remember that Vakhtangov used circumstances outside the context of the play to find the appropriate emotion. If an actor must enter in a state of fear, and the circumstances of the play are not working for him, he can imagine that a stalker is waiting for him in the darkness of the wings, or he might recall a particular piece of music that terrifies him, or he might fantasize that he is going to have a heart attack in the next three minutes. It doesn't matter, so long as what he uses causes goose bumps to run up the back of his neck.

Once on stage, however, the actor must respond to those around him, and to any change in the circumstances, and not simply ride the feeling of fear through the whole scene. Meisner calls the creation of this off stage emotion, "preparation"[11]

For Meisner, a preparation is completely individual. What works for one person, may not work for another. The point is to come on stage with something going on; with a full inner life. From there, the emotion will change depending on the circumstances of the scene.

The teacher cautions us that preparation does not have to be life or death every time. Sometimes, one is coming into a scene just to make coffee. An actor may not need an elaborate preparation every time. Do not, the teacher warns us sternly, force a feeling, or puff it up beyond its true size. If you do, the result will simply be bad acting.

What about on stage emotion, you may be wondering. We all admit that yes, we are wondering about that. Best of all, says our instructor, is when emotion flows spontaneously from your instinctive grasp of the character's circumstance. But when you run across a moment or a demand in the script that does not engage your instincts, you must use Stanislavski's *Magic If* (p.36).

Meisner's word for this concept of Stanislavski's is, *particularization.*[12] If someone in a scene calls you a "peasant," our teacher explains, and your character is supposed to feel outrage, you yourself may not feel it. In such a case, you particularize that moment by finding a label, such as "fascist" that would outrage you and act as if that person had called you a fascist. This use of "if" is one that actors often do unconsciously, our teacher says. But if you make it conscious, then you have a reliable tool.

Now what about handling the dialogue of a scene? Meisner likens the emotional life of the character to a river, and the text, he says, rides on top of it like a canoe.[13] If we carry this analogy further, we might say that the banks of the river, the boundaries that determine the river's direction, are the circumstances. This image makes clear that dialogue must come from feeling and circumstance. When emotion is truly flowing between actors on the stage, everyone involved, including the audience, can feel the "undercurrent."

One piece of advice that helps make such a flow happen on stage is to pick up the impulses, not the cues.[14] This means that you do not wait to react until the other person has finished their line. You must react with your face, your body, or with an action when the impulse occurs. The other person may be in the middle of what they are saying, and if your impulse is to nod in agreement at that point, do it. Don't wait to react until they finish speaking. You are obligated, however, not to say your line until they are done. This differentiation between impulse and line is crucial to the creation of a lively scenic interchange between the characters.

What then about character, we ask? Character, our teacher says, is simple and complex all at once. For Meisner, character is behavior. It is the "how" of acting. If a character does something slowly and carefully, we might describe him as cautious. If a character hits anyone who talks back to him, we would describe that character as a bully. Now that character might have good reasons for doing what they do, and that gives color and complexity to them, but their nature remains the same. Playing a character does not mean that you leave yourself behind. But it also does not mean that you are only yourself. As Stanislavski pointed out, an actor uses himself when he plays a character, and in order to make the character's behavior believable, the Meisner actor uses preparation and particularization.

As we leave class, we review some of what we have learned. Sanford Meisner's work is primarily aimed at creating a truthful exchange bewteen actors. He designs exercises that force actors to respond genuinely to one another, and to live spontaneously, moment-to-moment, within imaginary circumstances. His work deals with emotion without recourse to affective memory. But unlike Stella Adler, he does not dwell on actions, objectives, beats, obstacles and strategies. For him, this type of work can become overly intellectual and dry. Instead, he asks the performer to bring his unique talents and instincts to his class in the fervent hope that the student can become, through hard work, a more creative human being.

Today, classes teaching the Meisner technique are available in New York, Los Angeles, Seattle and other locales throughout the United States.

❊

Lee Strasberg, Stella Adler and Sanford Meisner all came to teaching from their work with the Group Theater. They were dedicated to using and extending the Stanislavski/Vakhtangov system and teaching it to American actors. Each flavored these ideas with his or her own particular ingredients, and each speaks of this work in his or her own dialect.

As a group, they have trained some of the most influential actors and teachers of the late twentieth century. And because of this, they have sometimes been regarded as gurus. Warfare has sometimes broken out between adherents of one teacher or another, and the teachers themselves have not been above personal attacks.

Defenders of a certain teacher may cite the great actors that have been trained by that teacher. The opponent may then cite the famous actors and directors that his teacher has trained. The truth of all this, is that famous actors have gone to many teachers in search of approaches that might help them. Robert Duvall studied with both Sanford Meisner and Lee Strasberg. Marlon Brando studied with both Stella Adler and Elia Kazan, and Robert De Niro Studied with both Adler and Strasberg.

❄

By the 1960's, the bickering had disillusioned many actors. In addition, a flaw surfaced in the work of these famous teachers. Actors trained by these men and women seemed unable to perform non-realistic material. Productions of Shakespeare's plays seemed to lack any sense of grandeur. Critics complained that actors domesticated Shakespeare's poetry and couldn't cope with his heightened prose style. Actors were accused of bringing Shakespeare's work down to a kitchen sink level. Some actors felt that the style of acting they had been taught was best suited to the intimacy of the camera. How were they to act in Absurdist plays, or anti-realistic material? Actors turned to improvisational techniques for a greater sense of spontaneity, and to Germany and to Poland for help in rediscovering the recently lost values of theatricality.

Chapter 8

Viola Spolin and the Theater of Games

At Hull House in Chicago, a woman named Neva Boyd began using games with the children of that city's poorer population. She discovered that play brought out these children's expressive potential and brightened their spirits. She soon saw that fun and creativity gave to them what their daily world often denied them: A sense of joy.

Viola Spolin worked with Boyd and developed her ideas further. Spolin created, at first for children and then for adults, what she called Theater Games. She saw that the Stanislavski system as it was being taught in the United States often bound actors up in over thinking and seriousness. The sense of playfulness, of play itself, was being lost. She realized that playing games was something grown ups had simply stopped doing. So, with a group of Chicago actors she began to explore the possibility of play with adult actors.

Some of the actors, including her son, Paul Sills, went on to found a company called Compass Theater out of which was formed the famous improvisational troupe, Second City. It is no overstatement to say that Viola Spolin is the mother of improvisation as we know it today.

❋

Our instructor gets us all up from our seats and tells us that we are going to take a ride on our bodies. He begins walking through the space and we follow. "You don't have to follow me," she says, "you can explore the space by walking in a different direction if you want." We disperse around the room. The teacher begins to talk to us.

"Wherever you feel tension in your body, shake it out. Put space where the tension is. Now imagine that the space itself is holding you up, that you don't have to do any work at all." We try this and it feels good. There is a lightness to us.

"Now imagine that only the bones of your skeleton and the muscles attached to those bones are holding you up, and that the space itself can no longer support you." Suddenly we feel heavy and we strain to hold ourselves upright.

"Notice," says our instructor, "that when you imagine that the space is holding you up, the strain disappears from your body and tension melts away. Relaxation of the body is what we're after. When you are relaxed, anything is possible. Keep walking."

"Imagine now, that the space is getting thicker. It is harder to walk through. Now, the space is thicker still." We find ourselves moving more slowly and with greater effort. "Now the space is so thick you can hardly move." We are barely moving. "This, by the way, is one key to moving in slow motion. All you have to do is move the way you normally would, but imagine that the space has thickened around you. Now the space is beginning to thin out." We begin to walk a bit faster, and our breathing is easier too.

"The space is almost back to normal. Now it is back to normal." We feel tremendous relief. But the teacher doesn't stop here.

"The space is becoming thinner, so rarefied that nothing stops your body. There is simply no resistance. Your body can move without restriction. You might fly off the earth if not for the gravity keeping you here." Everyone is darting around the room. But not chaotically, with control. After a minute of this, the teacher thickens the space back to normal. We are breathing hard.

"Now as you walk, with the space supporting you, look into the eyes of each player as you pass them, and say your name. In Theater Games, we use the term "player," instead of "actor" to emphasize the nature of what we are doing; playing." We say our name to each fellow player.

"Keep walking," says our teacher, "but this time look at everything around you, EXCEPT your fellow player." We walk and deliberately shut out everyone else. We look around them, never at them. It is remarkable how isolated and cut off we feel doing this. Amongst all these people, we feel alone.

"It feels better to be connected, doesn't it?" asks the teacher. We all agree that it does. Next, she numbers us in ones and twos. She asks each "one" to pair up with a "two." She tells us to stand opposite each other. We do.

"This," she explains, "is a mirror exercise. The 'ones' will initiate some movement and the 'twos' will mirror it back. 'Ones' don't move too quickly or the 'twos' won't have a chance to mirror you. After a while, I will say 'change.' When I say this, the 'twos' will become the initiators and the 'ones' will become the mirrors. After awhile, I will call 'change' again. I will do this faster and faster until I say 'follow the follower.' This will mean that no one is leading and no one is following, you will be on your own. 'Ones,' begin a movement, and 'twos,' mirror them."

Around the room people begin moving slowly, using their whole bodies. Their partners try to move with them as if they were mirrors. Some begin laughing and the teacher instructs them to stay with the exercise. Everyone looks very involved and focused on what they are doing. The teacher calls a change. Some of the couples are caught off-guard and lose their connection with each other. They soon readjust. The teacher calls another change, and the new initiator takes over. The teacher calls change again. Soon, the changes are coming so fast that we lose track of who is initiating and who is following. At that point, the instructor calls "follow the follower." The whole room is full of people moving in synch with one another. There are wild expressions on their faces as if they are about to fall off a tight rope. No one knows who is leading or who is following, but they keep moving. After a bit, the teacher asks us to stop.

"Very good. Fun isn't it? And hard. Did any of you feel that exhilarating feeling of following the follower?" Some say they did. "Good," says our teacher.

"Part of the point of these games, is to get you out of your heads. You have very little time to get bound up in too much thinking when you do an exercise like this, and that is good. It also connects you to your fellow player in a unique way. And connection also, is good." We think of Stanislavski's idea of "communion," and we think of Sanford Meisner as well.

"Following the follower, as you've just experienced it even if briefly, is key to improvisation. It is the flow between you and your fellow player that makes the games work. It is not your responsibility in a theater game to be in charge all the time. Sometimes you lead, sometimes you follow, and always you look to follow the follower. Don't fight each other, yield to one another. Good improvisation results from each player knowing how to give and how to take. If two players take all the time, they will talk over one another, never really listen and confuse the focus of the audience. If two players only give, their scene will lie flat and go nowhere."

The teacher asks us to sit down. We do. She then asks for two volunteers who are willing to try a two-person game. We raise our hand, and are chosen. Our fellow player will be a woman.

"Now, we need a 'who,' a 'what,' and a 'where' for these players," explains our instructor. The students call out all sorts of possibilities from their seats. We will be, it turns out, a psychiatrist and a patient, in a therapy session at the doctor's office. The teacher has thrown out some of the more exotic ideas, saying that simple relationships, actions and settings are usually the best. Then, she explains the game.

"This game," she tells us, "is called 'Jump Emotion.' And like all games, it has rules. This particular game is side-coached. Side coaching is when someone calls out an instruction from offstage. I will be that someone. If your voice is not being heard, a typical side-coach might be 'share your voice.' If you are speeding too quickly through a scene, someone might call out the side-coach, 'slow motion.' In this case, I will be calling out emotions. Your task is to jump fully to these emotions without thinking and express them fully within the context of the scene you are playing. So, let's recap." She turns to face the audience. "We have a psychiatrist and a patient in a session at the doctor's office." She turns to us. "Set up your 'where.' and quickly decide between you who is the doctor and who is the patient." She sits down. A few moments later, she calls out, "Curtain!"

The patient, who is the woman, is lying prone on the floor. We are seated in a chair near her. We both begin speaking as soon as we hear the word "curtain."

"Hold it," exclaims our instructor. "You've run into one of the biggest problems in all of this work right at the beginning, which is always a good place to start. Improvisation is not about talking, and it isn't stand-up comedy. It also isn't about playwriting. You do not have to jump to words right away. Remember to use your 'where.' What's in this office? Using the 'where' will save you from having to think up something clever. Which by the way, is not one of the rules of this game. The rules are to play the 'who,' 'what,' and the 'where' of this scene, and to jump fully to any emotion I call out. Being clever is not required. In fact, it would be a totally incorrect focus. Begin again. Get out of your head, and into the space. Curtain."

The woman stays in her position on the floor, but we go over to our space-desk this time (a real desk being unavailable) and pick up a space-pad and space-pencil (real paper and pencils are available, but the teacher has asked us to use space-objects only. Space-objects are, of course, imaginary things. And we are not to mime them into existence, but simply use them. (Sense memory helps us to do this).

We come back to our chair and sit, waiting patiently for our patient to speak. She says nothing. We wait. Still nothing. This could go on for days. Bored, we look around our space-office and see some space-books. We decide to get one. When we come back to our seat, we open it up. Our patient looks up at us, with a concerned expression on her face.

"Paranoia," calls out our teacher.

Slowly, the woman stands. "That's my diary, isn't it?" she asks. "What are you doing with my diary? You're not a real doctor are you? Why are you looking at me like that, my God, who are you, and why…"

The teacher interrupts her, calling out, "Give and take! You're just taking!" Our fellow player listens to this side-coach and stops rattling. We now have a chance to respond to her.

"Quiet, someone is watching us," we say. "Can't you feel it?" We both look around the room. She sneaks up on our space-desk and suddenly jumps at it screaming, "Come out of there!" But it turns out that no one was under there.

"Anger," calls out the instructor.

"Don't scare me like that," we say to the woman angrily. "This is my office, and you should be on the floor! Now lie down!" The woman comes up from under the space-desk and walks over to us.

"Don't order me around…" she yells. But before she can get another angry word out, the teacher calls, "Flirtatious." And without missing a beat she finishes the sentence in a sweet voice, "…you big therapeutic brute." Her hand is caressing our cheek.

"Why don't you sit right here on my lap," we suggest, "instead of on that cold, hard floor. It would be much nicer." As she starts to sit, the instructor calls out, "Silly!"

Instantly the woman plops down onto our lap.

"Let's play." she says.

"OK," we reply. We bounce her up and down on our lap and say in a sing-song voice, "This is the way to Boston, this is the way to

Lynn, hang on tight so you don't fall in!" At this we open our legs, and the woman falls through. We both laugh.

The teacher calls out,"Serious!"

We take up our space-pencil and immediately ask, "And this is the type of abuse to which you were continually subjected?"

"Yes it was," the woman replies. She gets up and straightens herself out.

"Interesting," we say as we write down some notes. The woman resumes her position on the floor.

"Sarcastic," calls out the instructor.

"Yeah," says the woman, "what's so interesting about it?

"Oh, don't you know," we say, "that it's just the most interesting thing that's ever happened. I mean ever."

The instructor calls out, "Happiness."

The woman clasps her hands together excitedly. "Oh really?" she says. The most interesting thing? For really real? I've never been interesting before!"

"Yes, very interesting," we reply. "You see I've been searching for years for a genuine nursery-rhyme neurosis, and you've got one!"

We rush toward each other.

"Thank you, doctor," the woman says, "you've made me the happiest neurotic on the face of the earth!" We embrace.

"Curtain," says our teacher. "Very nice. By sticking to the rules of the game, you found real expressive freedom. This paradox, that structure is freeing, is something you see all the time in acting. You both used the 'where' pretty well too, and you jumped to the different emotions with real commitment. At first, give and take was a problem, but after awhile you really seemed to be playing with each other. The scene you created had a real sense of spontaneity because you didn't think between each emotional shift, and because you didn't know what was coming next. You had to be in the present. Improvisation forces you to be in each moment with your fellow player fully, because the future is unknown. Poor improvisation results from trying to pre-plan your lines and responses. At that point, you are playwriting and no longer improvising."

"You may have noticed that many of the principles of Stanislavski were at work here. You had a circumstance to play which consisted of a 'who,' a 'what' and a 'where,' you had an objective, which was to follow the rules of the game, and you engaged in actions which supported that objective. But instead of approaching these ideas from the intellect, the game allowed you to get them into your body first."

"In acting classes we so often refer to what we do as our "work." And sometimes this refers to something heavy and ponderous. Theater Games help us to remember that a play is called just that; a play. And play is sometimes left out of our work as actors. Theater Games help us to remember the value of spontaneity and the beauty of the unknown. They allow us to explore a situation unhampered by the demands of a script, and they can reconnect us to our fellow players."

"And while Theater Games are the basis for most of the improvisational theater we see in this country, they are not limited only to that use. They are employed by some health workers as therapeutic tools in their work with deprived or disturbed children and adults."

"Spolin's contribution is a large one. Her approach has helped actors to rediscover the power of play in their work, and the surprising fertility of their creative imaginations. She died in 1995, and will be sorely missed."

Chapter 9

Bertold Brecht and the Theater of Politics

In 1956, the same year that playwright and director Bertold Brecht died, his theater company, The Berliner Ensemble, toured Britain. This company, from what was then Communist East Germany, so astonished the English-speaking community with its vitality, theatricality and unique style, that many felt an alternative had been found to both the stifling realism associated with Stanislavski, and the fake pomposity of the traditional English theater. The Berliner Ensemble conveyed strong political ideas using techniques derived from the circus, from cabaret theater, from the staging ideas of Vsevolod Meyerhold, and from the Chinese theater. Somehow, under the singular guidance of Brecht, all of these elements came together to form a unified sense of theater that transcended the sum of its parts. Suddenly, "Brechtian" style and "Brechtian" acting became the hot topic of theater people. How had Brecht achieved what he had? What were his thoughts and his methods? Well, as we shall see, his thoughts and his methods were sometimes entirely different things.

Born in 1898 in Augsburg, Germany, Bertold Brecht began writing plays at the age of sixteen (a play called, *The Bible*). It was thirty-three years later that he founded the company that so dazzled English audiences in 1956, The Berliner Ensemble. In the years between, he wrote and directed many plays and evolved a vision of the theater which he called, epic. So what, we ask, is this Epic Theater of Brecht's? (He later changed this name to "Dialectical Theater.")

When Brecht was a young man, the dominant style of acting in Germany was Stanislavski-based. The plays, too, were mostly realistic; well made and logical. But the young Brecht preferred the more radical works of Georg Büchner and Frank Wedekind. He was already writing poetry of an iconoclastic nature, full of irony, humor and sarcastic venom. Realism, which purported to be a copy of real life, held little interest for him.

Brecht felt that in the realistic style of acting the actors put both themselves and the audience into a kind of hypnotic trance. A trance that transported both audience and actor into a world far from their own, a world where they could comfortably believe in the illusion being offered, and leave the theater entertained and sated, yet numb to the social problems around them.

The whole process of the actor's identification with his part, and the audiences identification with the actor, appalled Brecht. Was the theater, he wondered, only a narcotic? An escape from the pain and struggles of the real world? Was the theater a place only to switch off one's brain and bask in a wash of communal emotionalism? We are reminded again of what Russian film documentarian Dziga Vertov said about realism in the cinema; that it clouds and befogs the mind (p.69).

Rather than the realism that he saw in the theaters, Brecht preferred the physicalizations of Charlie Chaplin and the Chinese actor Mei Lan-fang. These performers used physical gesture to illuminate the characters they played, and maintained a distance between the part and themselves.

If the audience was to be kept from falling into a collective dream with the actors, a separation between the actor and his role was not only necessary, but needed reinforcement. Brecht called on all the resources of the theater to keep the audience aware of its presence in a theater. By no means were they to be transported out of it. This idea, of course, flies in the face of the received wisdom that the theater should put audiences into what the poet Coleridge called, a "willing suspension of disbelief." Instead, Brecht is asking audiences to use their disbelief, exercise their skepticism, and resist the process of identification.

In order to achieve this distancing effect, Brecht adopted many of the techniques used by Meyerhold such as the half-curtain, placards announcing scenes, slide and film projections, music, narration, all in an attempt to disrupt the audience's tendency to fall into a dream. Just as they might begin to identify with a character, or become swallowed up in an emotion, an interruption is planned. A sudden song, or a slide projection on an upstage wall, or the appearance of a character in a mask, all serve to jolt the audience out of its stupor.

Now Brechtian language and terminology can be difficult. The usual name given to this distancing effect is "alienation." The actual German word is, *Verfremdung*, and sometimes this is shortened to *V-effect.* Most translators seem to agree that the best way to understand this word is, "making the familiar, strange." This really means that a common event or moment is performed in such a way that it can be seen with fresh eyes. Again, we are reminded of Meyerhold (p.68).

After Brecht became a believer in the political philosophy of Karl Marx, his goals became clearer. Rather than induce in an audience the relief of an emotional cleansing, he would create a theater that caused them to think and then incite them to action. Action outside the walls of the theater space. Action that would change the world itself.

Certainly as a playwright he could write plays that were aimed at accomplishing this goal, but Brecht, a practical man of the theater, knew that it was in the playing that a play has its true effect. How would the actor play in his plays? The crucial question became, what could an actor do that would distance the audience and yet still hold their attention?

First, Brecht knew what he did not want. He did not want the actor to empathize with, or transform into, the character. At least not in performance. He did not want the actor to look for the Stanislavskian logic of the characters' actions. Instead, he wanted actors to explore and heighten the contradictions in a character's behavior. "You look resolutely for contradictions, deviations from the typical, ugliness side by side with beauty and beauty side by side with ugliness."[1] This search for traits of opposites makes us think of Stanislavski (p.21). But whereas Stanislavski urges the actor to integrate character contradictions into a unified portrayal, Brecht wants the actor to highlight the contradictions without psychological explanation. Stanislavski wants to build a character, Brecht wants to explode it. But why?

One of Brecht's strongest objections to the Stanislavski system is its fixed view of a character. Because of his or her past, and because of present circumstances, the Stanislavski character arrives on stage fully formed and caught in a web of events. Choices are determined by the past, and the future is preordained. Brecht wanted audiences to see characters who were capable of different choices at crucial points in the action, points which he called "nodes." At these nodal points, the actor suggests to the audience that the character might make a choice which would produce a better future, and thus show each audience member that he too can change his actions for the betterment of his society.

But how does the actor accomplish this?

"To achieve the V-effect the actor must give up his complete conversion into a stage character. He shows the character, quotes his lines. He repeats a real-life incident."[2]

One of the most effective tools the actor has in playing this distance, is the adoption of an ironic tone. But this is sometimes overdone, especially outside of Germany. Many a performer has given what he thinks is a "Brechtian" performance by playing an entire part with a sense of wry irony. In the musical *Miss Saigon,* the actor Jonathan Pryce has been so accused. This tool should be used sparingly and balanced with many other elements.

Another tool the actor has is the use of what Brecht calls, *Gestus.* Like many of Brecht's concepts this term is difficult to write about. It is somewhat akin to Michael Chekhov's phrase, psychological gesture (p.66-67). The idea is to sift through many physical gestures until the actor finds the one or two that simply distill the essence of a moment or a series of moments. This gesture differs from Chekhov's however, in that it is meant not only to illuminate the character's inner life, but to comment on the social situation in which the character finds himself. One of the most famous examples of this is from the Berliner Ensemble production of Brecht's play, *Mother Courage.*

The character of Mother Courage is both an individual human being, and an embodiment of the greed of the capitalist class. The actress must present both of these aspects to the audience. The actress Helene Weigel found a particularly stunning Gest with which to do this. Mother Courage cannot be seen to visibly react to the shooting of her son by soldiers because this would keep her from continuing to do business. And yet she cannot be seen as so callous as to not react at all. She is a human being.

In one astonishing moment, when the soldiers are looking away, Weigel looks out at the audience, grabs her skirt, throws her mouth as far open as she can, and screams. Only she screams without sound. Her face is contorted with all the energy of shock and grief, but no sound comes from her throat. After a moment she composes her face, and collapses into herself. She hasn't given herself away; she can go on. In one moment the audience sees Mother Courage's inner torment and her ability to disguise it from those who might threaten her pursuit of the Almighty Dollar. The moment is made even deeper because the audience begins to see that Mother Courage "does not possess the ability to learn."[3] Thus, a personal and a social revelation are distilled into a silent scream.

And this brings up an important point. Does the actress playing Mother Courage actually feel the grief, or is she distanced from it? What is Brecht's attitude toward emotion?

In rehearsal, according to Brecht, a phase of the actor's work, is "the search for the character's truth in the subjective sense...You allow your character to react to other characters, to its environment, and to the plot."[4] This phase, where emotional identification is encouraged, follows the search for contradictions in the character. And it allows for the actor to empathize with his role.

The third phase of rehearsal, however, is one wherein "you try to see the character from the outside, from the standpoint of society."[5] When the part is finally performed, the actor's empathy for the character disappears. At least in theory. But as we noted earlier, Brecht's practices and his theories sometimes diverge.

Actors from the Berliner Ensemble report that Brecht seldom discussed theory with them. In rehearsal he was the practical theater director. He would watch a scene, make comments, send the actors off to work by themselves, and watch another scene. When the first actors came back, they would show Brecht what they had worked out, and he would accept or change what they had done. If they used real emotion sometimes, that was their business.

From time to time Brecht would help the actors to find the necessary distance from their roles by having them rehearse in the third person; adding "he said," or "she said" to the dialogue. But his main concern was the precise detail of the actions and the gests necessary to the production.

Brecht's goal as a playwright and as a director was to make audiences realize that history and society could be changed for the better. He therefore required of his actors a style of performance that could suggest different and better futures for their characters. In order to do this, the actor creates a distance between himself and his part so that he can comment on it. Yes, the Brechtian actor comments on his character even as he performs it. This, of course, is one of the great sins of most Stanislavski based training. But for Brecht, this is a crucial function of the actor. Without it, the audience would enter into an identification with the character and be transported out of the theater space and into some into illusory dream world.

But this does not mean that Brechtian acting should be devoid of realism. In this respect, his theories and his practice were at odds. He wrote to an actor in 1951, "To hell with my way of writing. Of course the stage of a realistic theater must be peopled by live, three-dimensional, self-contradictory people with all their passions, unconsidered utterances and actions. The actor has to be able to create such people."[6]

In the theater outside of Germany, it has been difficult to implement many of Brecht's approaches. Much bad acting and directing has been justified by wrapping the word "Brechtian" around it. Even in Germany today, with the collapse of Communism, Brecht is seen as old-fashioned. Productions of his plays are down worldwide. Many of the techniques of *Verfremdung* are seen everyday on television. Quick cuts, the jumbling of images, commercial interruptions of programs are commonplace. Today, instead of making the familiar strange, we make the strange, familiar.

In addition, it can be argued that the Group Theater's realistic production of *Waiting For Lefty* created as much or more social and political agitation as any play of Brecht's.

What can never be doubted, however, is the power of Brecht's challenge to Stanislavski. His work helps keep the actor from a rigid view of both his work and his value. His insistence on using the theater as a means of political change has influenced drama the world over. The epic comedies of Dario Fo and the Forum Theater of Augusto Boal are two current examples of the usefulness of Brecht's approach.

It is an easy trap to fall into, to believe that Stanislavski's and Brecht's methods are mutually exclusive. Many Stanislavski-trained actors claim great benefits from using Brechtian elements in their work, and many Brechtian actors have found great value in some of Stanislavski's techniques. These two methods need not be antagonistic, although Brecht might prefer it if they were. In the contradiction between them, he might say, an actor could find many treasures. And that would certainly be better than to have them melded into some unified approach which would likely dilute the unique power of each.

Chapter 10

Jerzy Grotowski and the Holy Actor

In 1959, a Stanislavski-trained Polish actor and director took a group of dedicated performers to a space in Opole, Poland and began doing research with them into the nature of acting itself. Jerzy Grotowski was dissatisfied with both the usual realistic approach to acting, and with the eclectic techniques of political theater.

Grotowski had done his homework. He had studied Stanislavski, Meyerhold, Chinese, Indian and Japanese theater. And his early productions reflected how well he had absorbed these many influences. But he felt the lack of an overall vision, a goal. Each production stood on its own and served no larger purpose.

In Opole, at a space called the Theater of Thirteen Rows, Grotowski began directing plays in all styles, from Eugene Ionesco's absurdist play *The Chairs*, to the classic Indian Kathakali play, *Siakuntala.*[1] He met great success with most of these productions and became a highly regarded director in his native country. And it was here that he began the experiments that would make him world famous.

Grotowski began to ask himself what theater really was. What, he wondered, was essential to its production? His answer was simple; space, actors and spectators. That was all. Theater could be performed without scenery, without props, without orchestras, without makeup, without lighting, even without a stage. But, "it cannot exist without the actor-spectator relationship..."[2] This stripped down theater, he called the Poor Theater.

He saw that on a technological level, no theater can successfully contend with the special effects available to the film and television media. So rather than compete in a realm in which it is sure to lose, he believed that the theater must offer only what is unique to it: Live interaction. The theater must rediscover its essence and present that to its audience. Grotowski wanted to focus on an aspect of Stanislavski's idea of communion (p.53) that also interested Brecht. Namely, the actor's effect on the audience.

But Grotowski wanted to go further than Stanislavski, and in a different direction from Brecht. He wanted to confront the spectator with the actor's ability to drop his social mask in the hope that the spectator too might find this possible. If the actor can contact an uncomfortable truth, the audience member might think that he can too.

To accomplish this goal, Grotowski focused on four areas. First, on the space itself; second, on the actor; third, on the spectator; and fourth, on the communal exchange among the three.

He knew one thing. He did not want to proceed by borrowing techniques from other systems or styles of theater. He considered this to be the "artistic kleptomania"[3] of what he termed the Rich Theater. Rather than clutter up the stage with gimmicks, Grotowski would strip it bare. The only music or sounds allowed would be ones that the actors themselves created.

The crucial step toward Grotowski's realizing his "poor theater," was his acquaintance with the ideas of the poet, playwright, actor and visionary, Antonin Artaud.

Born in 1896, two years before the founding of the Moscow Art Theater, Artaud forged a vision of theater that was unique. He rejected drama that was based on logical written text. He rejected drama that was based on the psychological examination of character. He also rejected plays that were political in nature. Artaud dreamed of something else. A theater that would show the mythological, the magical and the dangerous.

Artaud proposed a Theater of Cruelty which would purge the spectator of his murderous and anti-social impulses by seeing them played out on the stage. He wrote, "I defy the spectator...who will have seen...a bloodstream of images...to give himself up, once outside the theater, to ideas of war, riot, and blatant murder."[4]

How is this to be done, though, one wonders? What are to be the components of this theater?

It must be said that the two attempts Artaud made to actualize such a theater, failed. He provided little in the way of a practical program, and wrote in such a metaphoric and obtuse way that much of his thought is impenetrable. And yet some provocative ideas can still be extracted from his tortured mind.

After he saw a group of Balinese dancers perform in a forest just outside of Paris in 1931, he came to believe that the true job of the actor lay in his ability to make gestural signs. Now this sounds familiar. We immediately think of Michael Chekhov's *psychological gesture* (p.66), and Bertold Brecht's *Gestus* (p.151). We even remember back to Quintilian's body and hand positions (p.4).

But Artaud's idea is different. Quintilian's positions are meant to reinforce a rhetorical point, Chekhov's gestures are meant to illuminate the inner truth of a character, and Brecht's are meant to clarify social and political insights. The gestures Artaud saw the Balinese use were seemingly unrelated to any text, and bypassed the rational mind. They addressed the deeper realms of the unconscious, and for a surrealist poet, this was a familiar landscape.

Part of the Surrealist aesthetic was to reach beyond logic to the place where dreams live. No matter that Artaud misunderstood the gestures of the Balinese, they provided him with the conviction that the theater was the perfect place to present the magical, the irrational and the shocking.

Another, unlikely, source for Artaud's Theater of Cruelty came from the comedic films of the Marx Brothers. Artaud saw in them a delirious celebration of anarchy that illustrated his "...insistence on the necessary danger of the chance, disruptive event in his theater."[5]

So what might have a production of Artaud's Theater of Cruelty looked like? In Artaud's theater space, the audience and the actors would intermingle. The actors would wear elaborate costumes, and make sounds and gestures that would both frighten and awe the onlookers. Moments of pain might be interrupted by moments of laughter which, in turn, might be interrupted by musical shrieks. At least that is what one imagines. But Artaud's Theater of Cruelty never came about. He died in 1948 after having spent years in an insane asylum.

It is eerie to see him today in films like Abel Gance's *Napoleon,* where he plays the part of Marat, or Carl Dreyer's *The Passion of Joan of Arc,* knowing that he holds within his brilliant but unstable mind the image of a theater that he could not concretize. Watching him, we can imagine that he is still trying to wake us up, infect us with the fire of his vision, "signaling" to us, as he put it, "through the flames."[6]

❄

Of what use could Grotowski make of Artaud's scattered thoughts? First, his liberation of the playing space. Artaud showed that an area separating the actors from the audience was unnecessary. Actors could sit among the spectators, and even involve them in the action. This was a type of communion that Stanislavski never envisioned. Second, he saw "...myth as the dynamic centre of the theater performance."[7] But most important for Grotowski, Artaud saw that discipline and spontaneity "...far from weakening each other, mutually reinforce themselves."[8]

Like Artaud, Grotowski seeks a way to eliminate the separation between an impulse and its physical expression. For Grotowski, an actor must not impose thought between the impulse to action, and the action itself. In this sense, the actor must be transparent, without a filter. In a sense, he offers his performance as a self-sacrifice.[9] If the actor can accomplish this, the spectator may come to believe that he can too. Grotowski hopes, that in the intense interaction between the actor and the audience, a transformation can take place in both. This is what is sacred about his theater, and this is what makes an actor holy. But how is an actor to accomplish this task?

Grotowski approaches actor training from the direction of the negative; what he calls the *via negativa.*[10] Rather than asking the actor to do something, he asks the actor to resign from not doing it.[11] The idea is to give up resistance. For it is resistance, either of the body or of the will, that stands in the way of the direct translation of impulse into action.

The Grotowskian actor strips away, rather than builds up. This means that the actor must strip away the social mask he usually wears. This can make an actor uncomfortable. But he must give up his resistance, nonetheless, and go on. Grotowski understands that the actor's truth may make the spectator uncomfortable as well, but for that very reason it has value. The stripping away of the artificial always makes us uncomfortable at first. But later on we recognize that we have been enlightened.

In order to create an actor that can respond to the demands of his poor theater, Grotowski designed physical exercises that he called *plastiques.* They are meant to make an actor more plastic and strong. Grotowski's exercises address every part of the body, from the feet to the head. And he places tremendous importance on breathing and sound. For him, the whole of an actor's body should be a resonating chamber.

The actor must be a kind of athlete because the impulses that pass through him will often be large ones that require a strong, responsive, expressive body to contain them. But exercises, he cautions, are different from performances. They only prepare the actor for what is to come. And what is that?

Many have said that to know Grotowski's theater, one must experience it directly. Trying to describe it, they say, will only meet with failure. And yet, perhaps it is possible to give a glimpse of it if we use an example given by Grotowski himself.

Suppose, Grotowski asks, you are playing a character who must kill his mother. Now since you probably have not killed your mother, how are you to approach this action? Well, he wonders, maybe you have killed an animal. Perhaps you can use this experience to remember the sensory details, and translate these into the action of killing your mother. This is a common approach. But Grotowski says that using such a memory is not enough. It does not rise to the level of the event. It is too prosaic, too easy.

"Find something more intimate. For example, Do you think that the fact of killing...in this scene should give you a thrill, a sort of climax? ...If you want to say yes, seek in your own memories moments of intense physical climax which are too precious to be shared with others. It is on this memory that you must draw at the time of killing..." Imagine what a shocking moment this would be. It rises above melodrama and lodges in the psyche with tremendous power. The fact that there might be ecstasy in matricide is blasphemous. The discomfort it arouses is indelible. But Grotowski says that such a moment can free us all from the grip of our own murderous fantasies. By enacting it, and seeing it enacted, we are purged of it.[12] This example, of how to play a specific moment, helps us to understand how the Grotowski actor thinks. He looks for the heightened reality, for the taboo action that will jolt us into awareness. We share these shameful impulses, and we are united by our shame. And in this recognition of our common condition, we are cleansed. This is the theater of Grotowski.

❄

Our instructor stands before us barefoot. She asks us to remove our shoes and socks as well. We do so. She tells us that it is important to feel the surface of the floor. She then asks us to watch her. She stands for a moment and then launches into a series of connected movements. She loosens her body with twists and turns from where she is standing, she dives to the floor, rolls up into a shoulder stand, rolls back down, turns from side to side, then runs across the floor leaping in various ways. Now, she says, it is our turn.

We begin to twist our bodies as she did, we dive to the floor and then try to maneuver ourselves into a shoulder stand. We fail. The instructor comes over and helps us to achieve the right position. She then tells us to try it without her help. We cannot do it. She asks us to give up our resistance to the exercise, and we tell her we do not know how to do that. Go through, she says. Go through the resistance. Give up not doing it.

As we roll back into the shoulder stand, we feel our body tighten up, making it impossible to complete the move. At this moment our teacher tells us to relax the muscles. Go through the resistance, she says again, and this time we feel the muscles give way a little. Our shoulder stand is unsteady, but it's there. Good, says the teacher, go on. We execute the rest of the moves with the best of our ability. None of us, our instructor informs us, has done particularly well. We need, she says, to learn how to get out of our own way.

We work all day on various aspects of this exercise, even doing it in slow motion. In addition, we work on our voices. For Grotowski, our instructor explains, "bodily activity comes first and then vocal expression."[13] She does an animal exercise with us involving a bear and a trainer. The instructor plays the part of the trainer, while we are the bears. We let our bodies move before we vocalize. Sometimes the trainer is harsh with us and we let out ferocious roars, sometimes she tantalizes us with food, and we whimper and beg. Our movements are difficult, because we are unused to using our bodies in this way. Some of us give up and simply sit down. When the teacher sees this, she asks them to give up not doing the exercise. They get up and continue on.

The instructor makes clear that there is no perfect way to execute a plastique, no ideal form that must be filled. Rather, the actor uses the exercises to find his personal places of resistance. His task then is to confront them, and to resign from not overcoming them. That struggle is at the core of each moment.

At the end of the day, we have been pushed to our physical limits. Many of us feel that we cannot go on. This, says our teacher, is a crucial place to be. Have you noticed, she asks, that at moments of total exhaustion our inhibitions slip? That emotional expression is sometimes easier when the body is incapable of repressing it? We nod our heads in recognition of this.

It is at this point, she says, that our social masks begin to loosen, and that the deeper expressions of our being can come forward. The barrier between our impulses and their expression is thinner.

But of course, she explains, it is not nearly enough to simply be exhausted. Your bodies must be trained to actualize the impulses that flow through you, and you are all too tired for that. It is crucial for the Grotowskian actor to have an external technique powerful enough to articulate and embody the extraordinary demands made upon him. And there are many exercises and improvisations that help him to accomplish this. But they should only be attempted with a teacher trained in these techniques, warns our instructor.

In the 1960's Grotowski and his actors accomplished incredible things, our teacher tells us. Productions like *Akropolis, Dr. Faustus, The Constant Prince,* and *Apocalypsis cum figuris* changed world drama. By stripping away what was superfluous in theater, he helped to define its essence; the actor and the spectator, confronting each other in a small theater in Poland, hoping to find communion. For many members of Grotowski's audience, this happened. They report never having been so deeply affected by any other theatrical experience.

Grotowski's unique synthesis of Stanislavski's search for personal truth, and Artaud's vision of a transforming collective experience, created a theater of unique power. A theater that influenced Julian Beck's Living Theater, Joseph Chaikin's Open Theater, and the fascinating explorations of the great English director, Peter Brook.

In the 1970's Grotowski became more interested in one-on-one interactions with people, and staged no more productions at the Laboratory in Poland. But in 1983 he resurfaced at the University of California at Irvine with the Objective Drama Project. This was a project designed to study "...elements of performative movements, dances, songs, incantations, structures of language, rhythms, and uses of space...of various world cultures."[14] He called this, the Theater of Sources.

In 1986, Grotowski moved to Italy and founded the Workcenter of Jerzy Grotowski. There he worked on extending Stanislavski's *Method of Physical Actions.* He stressed "that the work on physical actions is the key to the actor's craft."[15]

Since 1992, he has been working on what Peter Brook has called, Art as Vehicle. In this work, the doer is the focus and not the spectator. In fact, there is no spectator at all. Instead, Grotowski is concerned with the "verticality" of energy. He wants the actor or doer to be aware not only of his body in space, but of "...something that is 'under our feet' and something that is 'over the head.'"[16]

Clearly, Grotowski continues to grow. He cannot be pinned down to any system, or any approach. He is a true seeker, and it gives his supporters a great deal of hope to see that this man is still dedicated to exploring the deepest ritualistic functions of art.

Chapter 11

Tadashi Suzuki and the Theater of Grandeur

Western directors and teachers have looked to the East since the time of Stanislavski and Meyerhold for new acting and directing techniques. Brecht was astounded by Chinese theater, Artaud was inspired by Balinese dancers, and Grotowski learned from the Peking Opera. But in one of the great ironies of history, it was when an Easterner saw performances from his own land done in a Western country that the theater found its next new direction.

In the early 1970's, the young Japanese theater director Tadashi Suzuki witnessed performances of the classical Japanese Noh theater being given in Jean-Louis Barrault's theater in France. Suzuki had seen many Noh productions in his own country, but it wasn't until he saw them performed in a foreign nation that their full power became clear to him: "I was made to recognize its superb theatricality. The rigorous training that had tempered and shaped the body of the actor produced a brilliant liveliness on the stage, right down to the tiniest details of movement."[1]

Suzuki's time in France changed him. His notion of what was possible in the theater expanded, and his creative imagination caught fire. When he returned to Japan he wanted to create a theater of unprecedented power and excitement. But the actors in his company did not show the stamina and concentration that he required. He realized that he would have to create a new kind of actor. There is nothing new in this. Stanislavski, Brecht, and Grotowski all expressed the need to train actors capable of fulfilling their different directorial visions.

Suzuki turned to the techniques of the classical Japanese theater, Indian Kathakali dancing, and even to Western ballet. His goal was to create an actor who, like Grotowski's actors could "make the whole body speak, even when one is silent."[2] Suzuki wanted "…to make it possible for actors to develop their ability of physical expression and also to nourish a tenacity of concentration."[3] And to this end, he created a series of forms that require balance, stamina, strength, and concentration, all in the service of a heightened theatricality and an expanded sense of actor presence.

Suzuki begins his training with the actor's feet. "The feet are the last remaining part of the human body which has kept, literally, in touch with the earth, the very supporting base of all human activities."[4] We remember that Michael Chekhov too gave great importance to the feet (p.75). Suzuki was, of course, also concerned with of the rest of the body, including the breath and the voice. But the feet and lower body seemed to him the root of the actor's expressivity.

Unlike Grotowski's exercises, Suzuki's do have an ideal form toward which the actor aspires. And it is this which makes the actor work ever harder, striving toward a perfection he can never achieve. In this way the actor must push himself forward, because his reward can only be in the attempt.

Suzuki turned his attentions to Shakespeare, Chekhov, and to the Greek classic plays and with his rigorously trained actors, particularly the brilliant actress Shiraishi Kayoko, stunned the world. His actors were capable of sustaining characterizations of tremendous intensity. The depth of feeling and range, the combination of expression and control, amazed and moved audiences.

In his productions the actors discover the greatest desires of the characters they play, and magnify them. So that in his production of Anton Chekhov's play *The Three Sisters,* the character of Irina has an epileptic seizure when speaking of her desire to go to Moscow. The powerful forces at work inside of her, joltingly externalized. In his production of Shakespeare's *King Lear,* the character of Edgar makes his first entrance already crazy. A Stanislavski-based actor might not move so quickly or boldly to this aspect of the character. He would let it unfold in a logical manner as dictated by the circumstances of the scene. But his offering might lack the impact and force of the Suzuki-directed performance.

In the early 1980's, Suzuki's work came to the attention of two men in Milwaukee; Jewell Walker and John Dillon. After seeing his work, these two invited him to America, and his influence has spread in this country ever since.

❄

WALKING

Our instructor asks us to line up against one wall of our training room and to cross diagonally to the other side. The walk we are to use involves an energetic striking of the foot on the ground which is best described as a stomp. The concentration, our teacher says, should be on the lower part of our bodies. With the upper half, we are to remain relaxed in an energized non-changing position. We are trying, she says, not to sway our upper bodies. This sets up an interesting dynamic between the two parts of our bodies. Our lower half is in constant energetic motion, while our upper half is still. Stillness and motion, two basic components of Suzuki training. Not opposing, but complementing each other.

The teacher leads us across the floor to loud percussive music. She is in a sort of squatting position, and we adopt this as well. On our feet we wear special cotton socks called, in Japanese, *tabi.* The challenge is to keep up the energy of our stomping without "loosening the upper part of the body."[5]

As we do this exercise, we realize that we must regulate our breathing, or we will never make it to the end. The instructor has also told us that the pelvis is the area which mediates the energy between the upper and lower parts of our bodies, and we remember to relax it slightly. The instructor has left us and now beats a stick sharply on the floor. At this sound, we change the nature of our walk.

This time we cross the floor up and back with our knees bent and our feet pigeon-toed. After this, we do the same exercise but this time we walk on the inside of our feet. Next, we shuffle across the floor, and finally we walk very low to the ground in a squatting position.

As we do these different walks, the teacher tells us not to stare, but to maintin a far focus, making contact with something outside of ourselves. As we do this work, she says, it is important to incorporate an inner task with the movement. This, she explains, helps connect the body to the emotional life.

At the end of another stomping exercise, we fall to the ground. The music changes to a beautiful and serene melody and we rise slowly. As we come slowly forward, each in his own way, we recite a series of lines from *The Trojan Women.* As we do this we keep our far focus and our concentration.

As we do these exercises we feel that we are gaining a measure of control over our bodies and find a special thrill in the fact that we have never moved in these ways before. We experience not only our bodies differently, but ourselves. The unfocused motions that we usually display in our acting are disappearing. We feel more confident in our use of bold movements, but also realize the power of stillness. It is as the instructor has told us before, that we must look for the stillness in movement, and the movement in stillness.

The teacher reminds us not to settle back on our heels, but to rest more onto the balls of our feet. She asks us if we are more aware of the energy in our bodies. We answer that we are. She asks if we are more aware of how to direct our energies. We answer, yes. She asks us if we are more aware of our bodies in space, and of the other actors around us. Again we reply that this is so. In fact, this training makes us feel more alive and present in every moment.

We have learned to execute what our instructor calls sitting and standing statues as well. These are exercises where we go up on our toes and hold a position. But even in that holding, she reminds us, there is movement. From this position we may recite lines from *Trojan Women,* or from some Shakespeare. Holding these positions and yet keeping our energy alive, challenges us almost beyond our limits. Parts of our body begin to shake from the physical strain. And we have been taught that strain is a central evil in acting. To be avoided at all costs. Certainly all the great acting teachers, from Delsarte onward have placed great value on relaxation, teaching that tension is the actor's greatest enemy. And yet, Suzuki breaks with this tradition.

For Suzuki, our teacher explains, it is the mastery over strain from which heightened emotion comes. How is one to play the high moments of tragedy if one is simply relaxed? No, says our instructor, physical readiness can be a great friend to the actor if it is used properly. The actor must be like a cat, ready to jump. But total bodily strain is not good, our teacher says. The upper body needs to be relaxed in order to speak, and the face too needs to be relaxed. In time, she says, the right proportions of strong support and relaxation will become clear to us.

The discipline involved in this training is rigorous. Once, she tells us, an actor held a position so long that a spider spun a web between him and the stick he was holding. At times we have had to overcome both pain and exhaustion in doing this work. But from it we have learned control. And with this control, has come a great confidence. Expressing large emotion with our whole body no longer intimidates us.

In fact, the style of realistic acting we usually see, now seems too small to contain the immense range of human expression that is laid bare in the great masterpieces of dramatic literature. Here perhaps is part of the answer to the failure of most Stanislavski-based actors to achieve success with Shakespeare. More seems to be required than *circumstances, objectives, communion, obstacles* and *actions,* although these are all needed. But a sense of grandeur, of power and control, an ability to find a heightened means of expression, these largely have been absent. Suzuki's exercises, we think, may help to fill this void.

The instructor seems to read our mind. She says that while most training in America has been psychologically based, that Suzuki attempts to train the total organism of the actor. A simple way to put it, she says, is that he connects the body to the head. He is bringing the intelligence and articulateness of the body up to the intelligence and articulateness of the mind. But, she warns us, that to see the exercises in production is all wrong. Now some Suzuki instructors, she says, disagree. But for her, seeing the training and not the character is simply wrong.

The more you use and apply these techniques, says our teacher, the more their beauty and power will reveal themselves to you. And remember, she tells us, Suzuki's work is always changing. So you too must be flexible. Don't worship the teacher, she warns, honor the work.

Chapter 12
Training School Profiles

Quintilian's mirror has been smashed. Today, few teachers place any importance on studying and copying gestures and facial expressions. And yet a strong danger still persists.

The mirror itself may be absent, but actors are now able watch themselves and others on screen. This can create a kind of self-consciousness about which Marlon Brando says, "Actors who watch themselves tend to become mannered. The less you think about how effective you are, the more effective you are. You don't learn to be effective from film, but from life."[1] So technology has brought the mirror back to us in a new way. How do we free ourselves from its seductive charm?

We must focus on the basic questions: How does one effectively persuade others of a fictional truth? How does an actor transform herself so that she can give passionate form to character?

There are many answers to these questions. For Stanislavski, the actor must enter the character's skin. For Brecht, the actor must hold the character away from himself like holding out a coat so that the audience can effectively judge him. For Grotowski the actor must strip away all artifice in an attempt to form a deep communion with the spectator. For Suzuki, the actor must contact a level of concentration and control that transcends the merely real.

But what is the real value of these different approaches? After all, acting isn't an intellectual exercise. Yet some of these methods seem to make it so. If a teacher is not careful, Stanislavski's work can become dry and overly cerebral. If a teacher only communicates the information of the Stanislavski system, the real purpose of it will be defeated. It should excite the actor, bring him joy and exhilaration. Brechtian style can be frustrating because no one really agrees on what it is. Grotowski's work requires tremendous dedication and teachers of his techniques are hard to come by. Suzuki's work sometimes seems only appropriate to his own productions.

All of this seems so complicated, such hard work. But acting should be simple, shouldn't it? Truth to tell, acting is simple. It is finding that simplicity that is so hard. For the highly talented of course, this search is easier. But not one of these teachers promises to make anyone more talented. The value they offer to us, lies in their ability to stimulate and direct our native gifts.

Actors need training no matter what their level of talent. In fact it can be argued that the more talent an actor possesses, the more technique he needs. So where does an actor turn for guidance?

In the United States today, actor training is divided between the private studios and the universities. The advantage that the private studios offer is that the student can take only the courses he or she chooses, and can study indefinitely. The universities offer the opportunity to put into practice what one is learning in the classroom through full-scale productions. There also exists, a kind of hybrid school, wherein a private studio links up with a university and they jointly offer a degree.

Let's take a look at some of these training institutions.

❄

ACTOR'S STUDIO/NEW SCHOOL
NEW SCHOOL FOR SOCIAL RESEARCH
ACTOR'S STUDIO M.F.A. PROGRAM

68 FIFTH AVENUE
SUITE 7
NEW YORK CITY, NEW YORK 10011
212-229-5859

Tuition is $16,040 per year.

The famed Actor's Studio has linked up with the New School for Social Research, to offer a program of training that results in the granting of a Master of Fine Arts Degree in Dramatic Arts.

The program is a three-year one divided as follows. The first year is called, like Stanislavski's book, An Actor Prepares, and focuses on the actor's work on himself. The second year, again following Stanislavski, focuses on Building A Character. The curriculum of this year for the actor's program is on beats and objectives. The work of the third year focuses on Creating A Role, which is also the title of Stanislavski's third book on acting. In this culminating year, works from the Playwriting track are acted and directed by members of the Acting and Directing tracks.

All students in the first year take the same program of courses. In the second year, the acting, directing and playwriting students separate, although some classes are held in common. In the third year, the students all participate in the creation and performance of plays.

This program features basic Strasberg exercises in relaxation, concentration and sense memory. In more advanced work, the private moment and affective memory are taught. In addition, the curriculum seems to indicate that some of the work of Sanford Meisner is included as well as some of the ideas of Stella Adler. In other words, the approach here is not as rigid as it might be at The Actor's Studio itself.

Along with the basic acting classes, the school offers classes in period style, theater history, movement and voice.

A feature of this program is the opportunity for all students to attend sessions at the Actor's Studio and to attend seminars led by some of the Studio's most successful members.

AMERICAN CONSERVATORY THEATER

30 GRANT AVENUE
SAN FRANCISCO, CALIFORNIA 94108-5800
415-834-3350

Tuition is $8320.00 per year for the M.F.A. Program.

The American Conservatory Theater is one of only a few professional theaters in the United States to offer a Master of Fine Arts degree in acting. The M.F.A. program takes two years to complete and a written thesis is required. In the next few years, ACT is looking to expand its training program to three years.

The training in the first year focuses on the actor's use of himself, his creative imagination and his voice, movement and speech. In the second year the student works on the use of heightened language and characterization. Also in the second year, more time is spent on performance.

In years past, company members of the American Conservatory Theater did the teaching. But recently, a core faculty has been developed here resulting in greater continuity. But a hallmark of this conservatory, still, is the opportunity to watch and to learn from working professionals.

The head of the Conservatory training program is Melissa Smith, former head of Drama and Dance at Princeton University and an M.F.A. graduate of the Yale School of Drama. She is also the core acting teacher for the second year students.

Jeffrey Bihr, a member of the International Company of Tadashi Suzuki, teaches Suzuki's work here; Frank Ottiwell is a Master Teacher of Alexander Technique in this program; Deborah Sussel teaches speech, scansion and dialects here; and Jeffrey Crockett teaches voice using methods derived from both Cicely Berry and Kristen Linklater. The fine actor Ken Ruta is in charge of student projects.

Some second-year students may be invited to be theater interns which may lead to an Equity card.

The program exposes the student to both classical texts and original works believing that both are necessary to the training of a complete actor. There is a strong emphasis here on language, and on the actor's ability to stay open to the many forms of theatrical presentation required by the many styles of world theater. A unique program offered at ACT is the Young Conservatory. This training is designed for younger people from ages eight to eighteen. Few institutions offer such a comprehensive young actor program which is headed by Craig Slaight.

AMERICAN REPERTORY THEATER
INSTITUTE FOR ADVANCED THEATER TRAINING
AT HARVARD UNIVERSITY
LOEB DRAMA CENTER

64 BATTLE STREET
CAMBRIDGE, MASSACHUSETTS 02138
617-495-2668

Tuition is $9,600 per year.

This two-year acting program leads to a certificate from Harvard University. A unique feature is that at the end of study, the student is put under an Actor's Equity contract. This is because of the close association of the training program with the American Repertory Theater.

The teachers are almost all members of the American Repertory Theater and include many graduates of the Yale School of Drama. Teacher Alvin Epstein in fact was Associate Director of the Yale Repertory. He is an actor of great stature, having appeared in Orson Welles' production of *King Lear,* and the American premiere of Samuel Beckett's *Waiting For Godot.* He has also directed many notable productions all across the country. Teacher Charles Levin is also a noted actor, with wide experience in theater, film and television. Film and television work, however, is not emphasized here.

The focus in this program is on the classic texts. The feeling is, if you can do Shakespeare, Aeschelus and Chekhov, you can do anything.

During the day, training involves instruction in the techniques of Stanislavski, movement based on Alexander Technique, voice based on the work of Kristin Linklater and Arthur Lessac, T'ai chi movement, yoga, combat, dance, singing and mask work.

Afternoons are given over to rehearsals where the acting students work with both directing students and visiting professionals. So an actor commonly goes from class to rehearsal to performance in a single day.

The reason that so many Yale alumni and teachers are now at Harvard, is that former director of the Yale Repertory and head of the School of Drama there, Robert Brustein, is now the Artistic Director of the American Repertory Theater.

CALIFORNIA INSTITUTE OF THE ARTS SCHOOL OF THEATER

24700 MCBEAN PARKWAY
VALENCIA, CALIFORNIA 91355
805-255-1050

Tuition is $14,600 per year.

The actor training program at Cal Arts offers both a B.F.A. and an M.F.A. in acting. Classes in voice (using the work of Kristin Linklater), movement (T'ai Chi, modern dance), fencing, combat, and textual analysis are central to the program.

Most of the acting teachers in this program are also directors. Their backgrounds are quite varied. Some have worked extensively in film and television, which is no surprise given the school's proximity to Los Angeles. Author, actor and director Robert Benedetti teaches here. He is the former chairman of the Acting program at the Yale School of Drama. Other acting instructors are graduates of the Cal Arts program itself, while teacher Lewis Palter was formerly the head of the acting program at Carnegie Mellon University.

The strength of this program lies in its diversity of approaches, its widely experienced faculty and its dedication to new plays.

While the basic concepts of Stanislavski are taught here, the faculty is expert at exploring other methods and techniques of the modern theater. In addition, students interested in working in film and television can participate in projects created by the School of Film and Video.

COLUMBIA UNIVERSITY
SCHOOL OF THE ARTS

305 DODGE HALL
NEW YORK CITY, NEW YORK 10027
212-854-3408

Tuition is $9,968 per year.

Columbia's M.F.A. in Acting is a three-year program and is influenced, like Juilliard's, by the French theater artist Jacques Copeau (1879-1949). Remember, one of the theaters that Harold Clurman greatly admired while travelling in France was Copeau's (p.82).

Copeau was less interested in Stanislavski-style realism than he was in "the richness of the many languages of theater." He wanted actors who could perform in whatever style was demanded by the text. To accomplish this, actors must be physically strong and flexible enough to meet the demands of the many styles of theater that exist now, have existed in the past, and will exist in the future.

Classes in movement, voice, speech, gymnastics and scene study are among those offered at Columbia. Improvisation in the tradition of commedia dell'arte, Meyerhold, Vakhtangov, and Artaud is also emphasized.

Columbia holds great interest for the acting, directing and writing student because of its faculty. Famed director Andrei Serban teaches here as does the celebrated Anne Bogart. Between them they represent some of the most innovative work being done in the theater today. Both are well grounded in the techniques of Stanislavski, but have explored new techniques and forms with excellent results. Bogart has worked with Suzuki extensively and was a guest speaker at his yearly Toga Festival in Japan in 1988.

The emphasis at this school is not on production. The philosophy of training at Columbia places greater emphasis on laboratory work than it does on large-scaled productions. And yet a great many shows are produced each year, and the student has ample opportunity to perform.

The excitement of the program at Columbia lies in the student's opportunity to learn from some of the most interesting theater artist's working today. Part of the philosophy of the school is that the acting students interact with the students in the other tracks including theater management, dramaturgy, directing, playwriting and design. So instead of highly segregated classes, students concentrating in specific areas have a chance to take some classes together and to interact on a daily basis.

HERBERT BERGHOF STUDIOS (HB STUDIOS)

120 BANK STREET
NEW YORK CITY, NEW YORK 10014
212-675-2370

Full-time tuition is, $1,666 per year.

HB studios is one of the most enduring private acting studios in the country. It was created by actor and director Herbert Berghof in 1945, but its greatest fame comes from the presence of actress and teacher, Uta Hagen.

Hagen was originally trained by Eva Le Gallienne (whose acting can be seen in the film *Resurrection,* starring Ellen Burstyn), and made her stage debut at the age of eighteen. She has appeared in many Broadway plays including *Othello, The Country Girl* (for which she won a Tony award), and *Who's Afraid of Virginia Woolf?*

In the fall of 1995, this remarkable woman returned to the New York stage playing the title role in Nicholas Wright's play, *Mrs. Klein.*

Uta Hagen is also the author of two excellent books on acting, *Respect for Acting* and *A Challenge for the Actor.*

As of this writing (late 1995) she is still teaching an advanced acting class at the studio. Her approach is Stanislavski-based, focusing on work with objects and with emotion memory. She draws on a vast well of experience and is a dynamic and insightful teacher.

The Studio itself, however, is more than Uta Hagen. There are many acting teachers there including actors William Hickey, Ann Jackson, Elizabeth Wilson, Amy Wright, Austin Pendleton, Laura Esterman and Arthur French. These teachers come from many different backgrounds. Some of them studied with Berghof and Hagen, some with Meisner, Milton Katsales, Mike Nichols, Kim Stanley, and Lee Strasberg.

The acting teachers focus on actions, objectives, circumstances, truthful behavior, concentration, imagination, sense and emotional memory and improvisation (Viola Spolin's Theater Games).

The classes are generally divided between beginning and advanced and these are further divided into technique classes and scene classes. A full-time student would be expected to take at least six classes per week, including beginning technique and scene study courses, speech, movement, and two electives.

The curriculum includes directing courses, classes in Shakespeare, Linklater vocal technique, Alexander movement technique, and yoga.

Getting into Hagen's classes and some other of the teachers courses as well, requires an audition.

THE JUILLIARD SCHOOL

60 LINCOLN CENTER PLAZA
NEW YORK CITY, NEW YORK 10023
212-799-5000 ext. 251

Tuition is $13,000 per year.

This school is one of the premiere training institutions in the country. Co-founded in 1968 by Michel Saint-Denis and John Houseman, the school is a combination of both of their approaches to acting. Saint-Denis was greatly influenced by the ideas and work of the French theater artist Jacques Copeau (1879-1949). Copeau felt that the actor's job was to serve the literary form created by the writer. He was less interested in realistic theater than in finding the proper style for each literary creation. Saint-Denis did not like the idea of "presenting a photograph of real life on the stage." The idea of an actor comfortable with the many styles of world theater was what he strove for, and this idea is still at the heart of the Juilliard program.

John Houseman brought to the school an American approach. He wedded to Saint-Denis' emphasis on style an emotional, inner approach to actor training. So the training at Juilliard is built on a foundation of eclecticism incorporating the views of two different traditions.

Today, Juilliard continues to train actors capable of bringing their inner life to the characters they play. They are encouraged to use themselves in order to transform themselves. This is key to the Juilliard approach. Actor's can only master different styles if they are able to meet the demands of that style while retaining an inner *sense of truth.*

The program is a four-year one leading either to a B.F.A., or a Certificate. Voice training is given nearly every day for the entire four years and Alexander movement technique is taught three days a week also for the full four years. Other movement classes are also taught, as is clown work. Moni Yakim, author of *Creating A Character,* and a teacher at this school, is a vital link in helping actors to accomplish the transformation that is so central to the Juilliard course of study.

In acting and speech classes, both the meaning and the means of language are explored. Because Shakespeare requires an understanding of the devices of poetry and rhetoric, scansion is taught. It is felt at Juilliard, that if an actor can master the classics, she can do anything.

Two of the acting teachers at the school are Michael Kahn, its current director, and John Stix. Both of these men are experienced theater professionals who have tested the many theories of acting on the stage.

John Stix teaches the first-year students and grounds them in some of the techniques of realistic training. He came out of the Yale School of Drama when its actor training program was dominated by proper posture and the clean delivery of lines. When he saw Strasberg's production of Odets' play *The Big Knife* in 1949, he wanted to know how the actors and director achieved their stunning results. Nothing he had learned at the Yale of that time helped him to understand how these people had achieved what they had. He very much wanted to understand their process. He became a member of the Actor's Studio and worked both with Strasberg and Kazan.

Over the years, Stix has winnowed out what he has found most useful in his approach to actor training, and what he has found less so. He demonstrates affective memory, but does not teach it. He does find sense memory, however, of tremendous value. His is not a doctrinaire approach. There is no fixed system, he believes, that can lay claim to the whole truth about acting. The teacher's goal is to bring out the unique talent of each student, and he uses many techniques to accomplish this.

School director and teacher Michael Kahn has made significant changes to the program over the last few years. He has created a playwriting track headed by writers Christopher Durang and Marsha Norman. This is of great value to the acting students because they have the opportunity to work on some of the new material created in this track. Kahn is looking not only to prepare actors for the theater of the future, but to help create it. At Juilliard he hopes to train theater visionaries who will create new forms of theater, and new ways to look at the classics. To this end he has brought in theater artists like JoAnne Akalaitis, and Ellen Lauren who teaches a six-week Suzuki workshop to the third-year students.

While Juilliard is committed to the great classic texts and to training actors who can perform them, the school is also open to the theater of the present and the theater of the future. The school has a core philosophy but is not doctrinaire in its application. At Juilliard the approach is eclectic without being haphazard.

THE NEW ACTOR'S WORKSHOP

259 WEST 30TH STREET
2ND FLOOR
NEW YORK CITY, NEW YORK 10001
212-947-1310

Tuition is $5,100 per year.

This new training institution was founded by three former students of the University of Chicago. They are, Mike Nichols, George Morrison and Paul Sills.

Mike Nichols, one of the original members of Second City theater, is one of America's premier improvisers and has eight Tony awards and one Oscar for the excellence of his directing. He teaches a weekly class, depending on his availability, for the second-year students. In addition to his training in improvisation, Nichols studied acting with Lee Strasberg.

George Morrison was also a student of Strasberg's. He has taught at the Juilliard school and has trained and directed some of America's finest actors. He teaches acting classes in both the first and the second year.

Paul Sills is the son of Theater Game creator Viola Spolin. He was a co-founder of the Compass Theater and director of Second City. He created *Story Theater* which has played twice on the Broadway stage. Sills teaches an intensive five-week course that culminates in a performance of a Story Theater piece by the second-year students.

This two-year training program is unique in that it gives equal value to Stanislavski/Strasberg-based training, and to the improvisational work of Viola Spolin. Balancing these two approaches is the focus of this school.

The school offers training in both Alexander and Feldenkrais body technique, speech, and Linklater vocal technique.

The student here must be aware that they may not get extensive work with the famous founders of this school, and that they will be taught by other faculty members. But these have been carefully chosen and have wide experience both as performers and teachers.

NEW YORK UNIVERSITY
TISCH SCHOOL OF THE ARTS

100 WASHINGTON SQUARE EAST
NEW YORK CITY, NEW YORK 10003
212-998-1960

Tuition is $19,000 per year.

The well-known program at NYU is a three-year one and offers an M.F.A. in acting. The first year of training focuses on freeing the body, voice, the emotions and the imagination. The classes are linked so that they reinforce each other. In the second year, acting work is focused on textual analysis and character development. Second-year students appear in productions throughout this year. In the third year, performance is the focus. Auditions are worked on as are other aspects necessary to the securing of professional employment.

Movement training features a great emphasis on Alexander Technique. There is no Suzuki training because it is felt to conflict with the Alexander body work.

Voice training is based on the work of Kristin Linklater led by Master Teacher of voice Beverly Wideman.

Speech training is taught by Deborah Hecht, Charlotte Fleck and Shane Ann Younts. These three have vast experience in dialects and in the International Phonetic Alphabet. Hecht and Fleck have studied with Edith Skinner.

Dan Cordle teaches Theater Games and Jim Calder teaches both mask and movement.

The acting classes are led by Mary Lou Rosato and the excellent Ron Van Lieu. Van Lieu is a student of former NYU teachers Peter Kass and Olympia Dukakis. In 1993 he won NYU's Distinguished Teaching Medal.

The Artistic Director of the Graduate Acting Program is Master Teacher of Acting Zelda Fichandler. She was the founder and longtime director of the Arena Stage in Washington, D.C.

The great strength of this program lies in its dedication to the vision of Peter Kass, one of the founders of the program, and his insistence upon training actors who posess a strong sense of personal presence. Zelda Fichandler has extended Kass's vision to include more work on the actor's transformation into character, but without losing touch with his personal uniqueness. This program aims to free both the emotional and physical selves of the actor.

Special offerings of this program are the circus class led by Master Teacher of Circus Techniques, Hovey Burgess, and the cabaret performances.

Recent NYU graduates have met with tremendous success in the professional acting world.

NORTHWESTERN UNIVERSITY
DEPARTMENT OF THEATER

1979 SHERIDAN ROAD
EVANSTON, ILLINOIS 60208-2430
708-491-3170

Tuition is $17,000 per year.

The fine reputation of this school is based on its undergraduate program. Northwestern does not offer an M.F.A. degree in acting. Undergraduates leave with a Bachelor of Sciences degree in Speech, and the curriculum is more academic than most. Within the School of Speech is the Department of Theater, and within the department, students can concentrate on the area of their choice in their last two years.

Many of the acting teachers here were students of the renowned Alvina Krause, whose very physical approach to Stanislavski influenced so many actors.

Acting courses are offered in a three-year sequence and focus on basic techniques, the study of plays, and the performance demands of different styles of acting. Courses in ballet, modern dance, jazz dance, gymnastics, and fencing are among those offered for physical training. Voice classes are required, and mime work is also taught.

Acting professor Erwin (Bud) Beyer is featured in Eva Meckler's book *The New Generation of Acting Teachers.* He combines elements from mime with the work of Stanislavski and Michael Chekhov.

The school emphasizes a complete liberal arts education, believing that the theater practitioner must be a student of human society and human behavior. But in addition to classes in the humanities, the Northwestern acting student has ample opportunity to exercise his performing skills in production. The M.F.A. directing students use actors for their projects, as does the faculty for the six mainstage productions done each year. In total, some forty productions a year are mounted in the various performing spaces each year.

Some special aspects of the undergraduate program at this school are the Children's Theater Tour and Participation Theater. The Children's Theater Tour offers actors the opportunity to experience the demands of a long run, and to explore the unique demands and rewards of performing for children. Students also have the opportunity to tour a show based on participation techniques. This is a style of performance wherein the actors and the audience interact. Northwestern is also part of the renaissance taking place in the art of storytelling.

Another interesting offering at Northwestern is the Certificate in Music Theater. This is a degree offered jointly by the School of Music and the School of Speech. The training combines courses in acting and characterization with classes in music skills, voice classes and music theater techniques. Actors interested in becoming musical theater performers are required to audition.

STELLA ADLER CONSERVATORY OF ACTING

419 LAFAYETTE STREET
NEW YORK CITY, NEW YORK 10003
212-260-0525

Tuition for the two-year program is $5,300 per year.

The first year of training at the Conservatory focuses on voice, speech movement, mask, improvisation, theater history text analysis and scene study. The second year continues training in voice and movement and physical acting. Styles like Shakespeare and film and television acting are also covered in this year.

Classes in acting technique follow Adler's concern with actions, circumstances, justifications, subtext, and character elements.

The program is affiliated with New York University's Tisch School of the Arts, and offers a B.F.A. in acting.

Most of the acting-technique teachers here were trained by Stella Adler herself, and this gives a vision of continuity to the various classes. Perhaps the best-known professional teaching at the Conservatory is Broadway actress Elaine Stritch.

One of the interesting features of the program is the use of mask work. Students begin with what is known as the neutral mask and then move on to character masks. This training teaches the actor many things. For one, it forces him to be expressive with his body, and for another it helps him to affect the transformation into character.

Stella Adler died in 1992.

UNIVERSITY OF ILLINOIS URBANA-CHAMPAIGN

DEPARTMENT OF THEATER
KRANNERT CENTER FOR THE PERFORMING ARTS
URBANA, ILLINOIS 61801
217-333-2371

Tuition for residents is $3,750 per year.

Tuition for non-residents is $9,620 per year.

The M.F.A. program here takes three years to complete. The first semester covers improvisation and Stanislavski's methods as they apply to the plays of Anton Chekhov.

In the second semester Stanislavski's techniques are applied to other playwrights. Mask work and clowning are also offered.

Second- and third-year students work on specialties such as musical theater, comedy, Shakespeare, or acting for the camera.

The Acting training is headed by teacher and director David Knight. He was a Fulbright student in England at the Royal Academy of Dramatic Art and stayed in England, working as an actor in every venue, for twenty years. A strong offering at this University is the film and television work that Knight does. Few teachers have as much experience in this area as he does.

Voice, speech, and combat are also mainstays of this program.

The program is affiliated with the Illinois Repertory Theater of which David Knight is the Artistic Director.

UNIVERSITY OF WASHINGTON

SCHOOL OF DRAMA DX-20
SEATTLE, WASHINGTON 98195
206-543-5140

Tuition for non-resident Undergraduates is $6,345.

Tuition for non-resident Graduates is $8,850.

Tuition for resident Undergraduates is $2,253.

Tuition for resident Graduates is $3,537.

The Professional Actor Training Program is a three-year one that culminates in the awarding of an M.F.A. Degree.

This program has attracted a lot of attention in recent years because of its attempt to combine the teachings of Stanislavski with the work of Tadashi Suzuki. The presence of Suzuki's work is due to the fact that former University of California at San Diego teacher Steven Pearson, has been appointed head of actor training here.

Graduate students are trained in the techniques of Suzuki and bring that work into their scene study in studio. There the work is integrated with character intentions, dramatic circumstances and character demands.

This is one of the few places in the United States where Suzuki's work is systematically taught, and the graduate training program is considered by many to be one of the finest in the country.

Voice work is taught by Judith Shahn who is trained in the work of Kristin Linklater.

The Undergraduate Department integrates the work of Stanislavski with the work of Suzuki under the excellent guidance of teacher Robyn Hunt.

UNIVERSITY OF WISCONSIN AT MILWAUKEE

PROFESSIONAL THEATER TRAINING PROGRAM
P.O. BOX 413
MILWAUKEE, WISCONSIN 53201
414-229-4947

Tuition for residents in Graduate Study is $3,870 per year.

Tuition for residents in Undergraduate studies is $2,772 per year.

Tuition for non-residents in Graduate study is $11,536 per year.

Tuition for non-resident in Undergraduate study is $8,786 per year.

The program at this University offers both a B.F.A. and an M.F.A. in acting. Both Feldenkrais and Alexander movement techniques are available here, and voice and speech is taught by author and director Malcolm Morrison. He was Dean of the School of Drama at the North Carolina School of the Arts.

The M.F.A. program is a three-year one and is particularly strong on the physical side of acting technique. Combat teacher Richard Raether is one of only nine who are certified by the Society of American Fight Directors.

This program is one of the few that focuses on the speaking of verse. Other programs give this skill some attention, but here, it is given more importance.

In all three years, the students are involved in production and so have an opportunity to try out their newly won skills.

The Professional Training Program is affiliated with the Northern Stage Company so students have the chance to work alongside experienced professionals.

A unique feature of this program is that members of the training program have the opportunity to perform in different countries around the world through the World Theater Training Institute of which Malcolm Morrison is the president.

YALE UNIVERSITY

SCHOOL OF DRAMA
P.O. BOX 208325
NEW HAVEN, CONNECTICUT 06520-8325
203-432-1507

Tuition is $12,950 per year.

This program offers an M.F.A. Degree after three years of study.

The first year of study focuses on realistic acting. This means that the basic techniques of Stanislavski are explored including actions, circumstances and objectives. Voice, speech, movement, are constants throughout the training program. Fencing is part of the work of the first year and mask work is done in the first and second years.

In the second year, the demands of verse are explored. Scenes from Shakespeare are used for study and mime, stage combat and singing are included in the curriculum.

Third year students focus on contemporary acting styles and some may be invited to perform with the Yale Repertory Theater. In this year the student combines the skills he has learned and applies them to production.

The Yale University School of Drama is one of the most illustrious training institutions in the United States. Actors who have completed training here can confidently expect that hiring professionals will be interested in them.

Robert Lewis taught here from the years 1967 to 1976 when he helped to train such luminaries as Meryl Streep, Sigourney Weaver, Henry Winkler and Jill Eikenberry. His emphasis on a seamless melding of inner and outer technique is still a hallmark of this school.

Conclusions

So, is acting done from the outside in, or the inside out?

We realize now, that this question is nonsense. Without an outer technique, the actor has no way to express his inner life. And without an inner technique, the actor has nothing to say. If we agree on this, what then accounts for the heated disputes about acting and how it should be taught?

What was once a discovery based on living truth, can all too often become petrified dogma. If Delsarte raises his hand in a particularly effective way while expressing fear, why then must everyone do the same, believing that the magic is in the gesture alone. This is only human nature. If a favorite basketball player wears a certain brand of shoe, we want to wear it also, believing that our skills will be like his if we wear what he does. In the same way, actors imitating only the external results of a great actor will almost certainly fail to find for themselves that actor's greatness.

The performing style that Stanislavski rebelled against was just this sort of imitated external acting; a style that possessed great power in the hands of David Garrick, but not in his imitators.

Stanislavski fought to create a new style of acting that could be newly felt and communicated each and every night. A style that would avoid cliché and reach deep into the soul of the audience. Unfortunately, the genuine realism that Stanislavski began could also be imitated. Realism came to stand for a casual and banal acting style that was light years away from the energy and creativity that Stanislavski initially unleashed. In many hands, realism itself became a cliché

Vakhtangov, Meyerhold, and Brecht each tried to breathe theatricality back into the actor's life. They did this mostly by addressing gesture, movement and voice; by rediscovering the body. Today, Jerzy Grotowski and Tadashi Suzuki are at the forefront of this renewed focus on physicality.

But this focus is different from that prescribed by Quintilian or Aaron Hill or Delsarte. Today's body-oriented teachers presuppose that an inner technique is in place. The mind-body connection is critical to them and they expect it to be there. Without passionate, detailed involvement of the actor's inner life, they realize that physical expression is hollow; a shadow of a pose, and believable transformation cannot take place.

Many schools, both private studios and University programs, try to address this problem by balancing movement, voice and mask work with the principles and methods of realism. The question the student must ask, then, is how well integrated are the classes in external technique with the ones in internal technique? Often these classes have little to do with one another and the actor leaves with many separate skills that do not mesh.

Actor training is highly teacher-dependent. Most teachers have the information about acting but not many are greatly gifted at communicating it. And ultimately, acting isn't about the information, anyway. The teacher must communicate the madness of the art, the passion for the craft, the excitement of inspiration.

There must be joy and hard work in it all. Stanislavski once said, "A teacher who introduces an atmosphere of fear and trembling into the studio...should not be allowed to teach in it."[1] This is not to say that the student should only be told positive things. Criticism and sometimes shock are of great value in an acting class. But the student must assess if he is being cowed and intimidated on a constant basis, or if he is being inspired and brought forward. Unfortunately the only way a student can gauge this is by being in the classroom with the instructor.

While an attempt is being made today to bring the body back into acting, one wonders if this is happening just to attract students and to stay competitive, or because there exists a real vision of what an actor should be.

It is the personal opinion of this writer that there has never been, and is not now, any consistent or agreed upon view in this country of what an actor should be. When a teacher or director with a unique vision does appear, his or her work runs through the acting community like a fever, and then usually disappears. One thinks in this regard of the Grotowski movement of the late 1960's and early 1970's, of which there is today, little trace. One wonders if this same fate will meet the work of Tadashi Suzuki.

Perhaps it is good that no single acting training curriculum exists. If it did, the great variety of approaches might be narrowed and the teaching of acting become petrified. And yet, one does feel the need for some overarching passionate vision to which every actor could dedicate himself. Where is such an articulate, inspiring and clear view of the nature and purpose of acting? In the 1930's, Harold Clurman provided it for the Group Theater.

Where is such a voice today?

Is it yours?

ENDNOTES

INTRODUCTION

1. Plutarch, *The Rise and Fall of Athens: Nine Greek Lives,* trans. Ian Scott-Kilvert, Viking Penguin Inc., New York, 1960, p. 63.

CHAPTER 1

1. Quintilian, quoted by Joseph R. Loach, *The Player's Passion,* University of Michigan Press, 1993, p.24.
2. Aaron Hill quoted by Edwin Duerr in *The Length and Depth of Acting,* Holt, Rinehart and Winston, Inc., 1962, p.222.
3. Shawn, Ted. *Every Little Movement,* M. Witmark & Sons, N.Y., 1963, p.16.
4. Stebbins, Genevieve. *Delsarte System of Dramatic Expression,* Edgar S. Werner, N.Y., 1886, p.40.
5. Ibid., p.118.
6. Ibid., p.229.
7. Ibid., pp.62-63.
8. Quoted by Ted Shawn in *Every Little Movement,* M. Witmark & Sons, N.Y., 1963, p.57.
9. James, William and Lange, Carl. *The Emotions,* Hafner Publishing Co., N.Y., 1967, p.13.
10. Stebbins, Genevieve. *Delsarte System of Dramatic Expression,* Edgar S. Werner, N.Y., 1886, p.63.
11. Ibid., p.11.
12. Ibid., p.11.
13. Ibid., p.63.
14. Shawn, Ted. *Every Little Movement,* M. Witmark & Sons, N.Y., 1963, p.18.
15. Denis Diderot quoted by Edwin Duerr in *The Length and Depth of Acting,* Holt, Rinehart, and Winston, Inc., 1962, p.265.
16. Luigi Riccoboni quoted by Edwin Duerr in *The Length and Depth of Acting,* Holt, Rinehart, and Winston, Inc., 1962, p.214.

CHAPTER 2

1. Stanislavsky, Constantine. *My Life In Art,* translated by J.J. Robbins, Little, Brown and Company, 1924.
2. Ibid., p.61.

3. Quoted by Christine Edwards in *The Stanislavsky Heritage.* New York University Press, N.Y., 1965, pp.15-16.
4. Stanislavsky, Constantine. *My Life In Art,* translated by J.J. robbins, Little, Brown and Company, 1924, p.88.
5. Ibid., p.76.
6. Ibid., p.90.
7. Ibid., p.158.
8. Ibid., p.184.
9. Ibid., p.182.
10. Ibid., p.182.
11. Magarshack, David. *Stanislavsky A Life,* Faber and Faber Ltd., London, 1986, p.152-3.
12. Ibid., p.155
13. Ibid., p.168
14. Gordon, Mel. *The Stanislavsky Technique: Russia.* Applause Theater Book Publishers, N.Y., p.22.
15. Stanislavsky, Constantine. *An Actor Prepares.* Translated by Elizabeth R. Hapgood, Routledge / Theater Arts Books, NY, 1988, p.81.
16. Ibid., p.82.
17. Gordon, Mel. *The Stanislavsky Technique: Russia.* Applause Theater Book Publishers, N.Y., p.62.
18. Stanislavsky, Constantine. *An Actor Prepares.* Translated by Elizabeth R. Hapgood, Routledge / Theater Arts Books, NY, 1988, p.164.
19. Ibid., p.185.
20. Plato, quoted in *Actors On Acting.* Edited by Toby Cole and Helen Krich Chinoy, Crown Publishers, Inc., NY, 1970, p.7.
21. Based on information from *Stanislavsky A Biography,* by Jean Benedetti. Routledge, NY, 1988, p.180.
22. Based on information from *Method Or Madness,* by Robert Lewis. Samuel French, Inc., N.Y., 1986.
23. Gordon, Mel. *The Stanislavsky Technique: Russia.* Applause Theater Book Publishers, N.Y., p.239.

CHAPTER 3

1. Quoted in *Daily Life In Russia under the Last Tsar,* by Henri Troyat. Stanford University Press, Stanford, Calif., 1959, p.44.
2. In his book *The Theater Event,* author Timothy J. Wiles points out that while Elizabeth Reynolds Hapgood translates the phrase as, "living the role," the author and translator Burnet M. Hobgood more accurately translates it as, "experiencing the role." University of Chicago Press, Chicago, 1980, pp.191-2.

3. Vakhtangov quoted by Nikolai Gorchakov in *The Vakhtangov School of Stage Art.* Trans. by Ivanov-Mumjiev, edited by Phyl Griffith, Foreign Languages Publishing House, Moscow, p.40.
4. Vakhtangov, Evgeni quoted in *Directors On Directing,* edited by Toby Cole and Helen Chinoy, Bobbs-Merrill, Indianapolis, 1953, p.185.
5. Gordon, Mel. *The Stanislavski Technique: Russia,* Applause Theater Book Publishers, N.Y., 1987, p.83.
6. Strasberg, Lee. *Russian Notebook* (1934), The Drama Review, Volume 17 Number 1(T-57), March, 1973, New York University, N.Y., p.110.
7. Benedetti, Jean. *Stanislavski, A Biography,* Routledge, N.Y., 1988, p.249.
8. Moore, Sonia. *The Stanislavski System,* Penguin Books, N.Y., 1965, p.102.
9. Gordon, Mel. *The Stanislavski Technique: Russia,* Applause Theater Book Publishers, N.Y., 1987, p.121.
10. Chekhov, Michael, *On The Technique of Acting,* HarperCollins Publishers, N.Y., p.26.
11. Chekhov, Anton. *The Cherry Orchard.* Translated by Ann Dunigan, Signet-New American Library, 1964, p.315.
12. Chekhov, Michael. *Lessons for the Professional Actor.* Performing Arts Journal Publications, N.Y., 1992, p.133
13. Benedetti, Jean. *Stanislavski A Biography,* Routledge, N.Y., 1988, p.171.
14. Quoted in, *The Film Factory-Rusian and Soviet Cinema in Documents 1896-1939.* Edited and translated by Richard Taylor, coedited by Ian Christie, Harvard University Press, Mass., 1988 p.69.
15. Ibid., p.116.
16. Duerr, Edwin. *The Length and Depth of Acting.* Holt, Rinehart and Winston, N.Y., 1962, p.471.
17. From the March 1973 edition of *The Drama Review,* Volume 17 Number 1, Lee Strasberg's Russian Notebook (1934), p.111.
18. Gordon, Mel. *Meyerhold's Biomechanics,* in Acting (Re)Considered, Edited by Phillip B. Zarrilli, Routledge, N.Y., 1995, p.95.
19. Braun, Edward, *Meyerhold On Theater.* Hill and Wang, N.Y., 1969, p.251.

CHAPTER 4

1. Garfield, David. *A Player's Place.* MacMillan Publishing Co., Inc, N.Y., 1980, p.15.
2. Hull, S. Loraine. *Strasberg's Method,* Ox Bow Publishing, Inc., Conn., 1985, p.161.
3. Willis, Ronald A. *The American Lab Theater,* in Tulane Drama Review, Volume 9, Number 1, Fall, 1964, p.113.
4. Smith, Wendy. *Real Life Drama.* Grove Weidendeld, N.Y., 1990, p.8.

5. Ibid., p.37.
6. Ibid., p.37.
7. Ibid., p.61.
8. Ibid., p.91.
9.Ibid., p.181. A quote from Robert Lewis.
10.Gray, Paul quoting Sanford Meisner in Tulane Drama Review volume 9 number 2, Winter, 1964, in an article entitled *Stanislavski and America: A Critical Chronology,* p.35.

CHAPTER 5
1. Brando, Marlon. Brando, *Songs My Mother Taught Me,* Random House, N.Y., 1994, p.85.
2. Strasberg quoted in an interview conducted by Richard Schechner in *Working With Live Material,* from the Tulane Drama Review, volume 9, number 1, Fall, 1964, p.121.
3. Ibid., p.121.
4. Ibid., p.121.
5. Hull, S. Loraine. *Strasberg's Method,* Ox Bow Publishing, Inc., Conn., 1985, pp.77-78.
6. Miller, Allan. *A Passion For Acting,* Back Stage Books, N.Y., 1992, p.122.
7. Strasberg quoted in an interview conducted by Richard Schechner in *Working With Live Material,* from the Tulane Drama Review, volume 9, number 1, Fall, 1964, p.132.
8. Robert Lewis quoted in *Strasberg's Method* by S. Loraine Hull, Ox Bow Publishing, Inc.,Conn., 1985, p.96.

CHAPTER 6
1. Adler, Stella, *The Technique of Acting.* Bantam Books, N.Y., 1988, p.11.
2. Ibid., p.16.
3. Ibid., p.26.
4. Ibid., p.35.
5. Ibid., p.75
6. Ibid., p.102.
7. Ibid., p.103

CHAPTER 7
1. Smith, Wendy. *Real Life Drama,* Grove Weidenfeld, N.Y., 1990, p.206, concerning Meisner's performance in Awake and Sing.
2. Gray, Paul. *The Reality of Doing,* Tulane Drama Review Volume 9, number 1, Fall, 1964, p.139.

3. Meisner, Sanford and Dennis Longwell, *Sanford Meisner On Acting.* Random House, Inc. N.Y., 1987, p.11.
4. Ibid., p.15.
5. Ibid., p.59.
6. Silverberg, Larry. *The Sanford Meisner Approach,* Smith and Kraus, Lyme, N.H., 1994, p.14.
7. Ibid., p.17.
8. Ibid., p.51.
9. Ibid., p.52.
10. Meisner, Sanford and Dennis Longwell. *Sanford Meisner On Acting,* Random House, Inc., N.Y., 1987, p.40.
11. Ibid., p.78.
12. Ibid., p.138.
13. Ibid., p.115.
14. Ibid., p.73.

CHAPTER 9

1. Brecht, Bertold. *Notes on Stanislavski,* Quoted in Tulane Drama Review, Volume 9, number 2, Winter, 1964, p. 159.
2. Brecht, Bertold quoted by Peter Brooker in *Key Words in Brecht's Theory and Practice,* from The Cambridge Companion To Brecht, edited by Peter Thomson and Glendyr Sacks, Cambridge University Press, NY, 1994, p.197.
3. Weigel, Helene. quoted in *Notes On Stanislavski,* by Bertold Brecht in Tulane Drama Review, Volume 9 number 2, Winter, 1964, p. 163.
4. Brecht, Bertold, *Notes on Stanislavski.* Quoted in Tulane Drama Review, Volume 9, number 2, Winter, 1964, p. 159.
5. Ibid., p. 159.
6. Brecht, Bertold, trans. and ed. by John Willet, *Brecht On Theater,* Hill and Wang, N.Y., 1992, p. 235.

CHAPTER 10

1. Wiles, Timothy J. *The Theater Event,* University of Chicago Press, 1980, p.139.
2. Grotowski, Jerzy. *Towards A Poor Theater.* Simon and Schuster, Inc., N.Y., 1968, p.19.
3. Ibid., p. 19.
4. Artaud, Antonin, quoted in *The Theater Event* by Timothy J. Wiles. University of Chicago Press, 1980, p. 136.

5. Wiles, Timothy J. *The Theater Event.* University of Chicago Press, 1980, p. 46.
6. Artaud, Antonin. *The Theater And Its Double,* trans. Mary Caroline Richards, Grove Press, N.Y., 1958, p.13.
7. Grotowski, Jerzy. *Towards A Poor Theater,* Simon and Schuster, Inc., N.Y., 1968, p.121.
8. Ibid., p.121.
9. Ibid., p.43.
10. Ibid., p.17.
11. Ibid., p.17
12. Ibid., p.233-34
13. Ibid., p.183.
14. I. Wayan Lendra quoting Dr. Robert Cohen in *Bali and Grotowski,* in the book *Acting (Re)Considered,* edited by Phillip Zarrilli, Routledge, N.Y., 1995, p.137.
15. Richards, Thomas. *At Work With Grotowski on Physical Actions,* Routledge, N.Y., 1995, p. 31.
16. Grotowski, Jerzy, *At Work With Grotowski on Physical Actions,* by Thomas Richards, Routledge, NY, 1995, p.125.

CHAPTER 11

1. Suzuki, Tadashi. *The Way of Acting,* trans. J. Thomas Rimer, Theater Communicaions Group, N.Y., 1986, p.71.
2. Suzuki, Tadashi. *Culture is the Body,* in *Acting (Re)Considered,* edited by Phillip Zarrilli, Routledge, N.Y., 1995, p.155.
3. Ibid., p.155.
4. Ibid., p.160.
5. Suzuki, Tadashi. *The Way of Acting,* trans. J. Thomas Rimer, Theater Communications Group, N.Y., 1986, p.9.

CHAPTER 12

1. Marlon Brando, quoted by Brian Bates in *The Way of the Actor,* Shambhala Publications, Inc., Boston, Mass., 1987, p.115.

CONCLUSIONS

1. Constantine Stanislavski quoted by Davis Magarshack in *Stanislavski on the Art of the Stage,* trans. David Magarshack, Faber and Faber, Limited, Boston, Mass., 1950, p. 126.

BIBLIOGRAPHY

GENERAL ACTING

Bates, Brian. *The Way of the Actor.* Shambhala Publications, Inc., Boston, 1987.

Callow, Simon. *Being An Actor.* Grove Press, N.Y., 1984.

Cole, Toby and Helen Krich Chinoy, ed. *Actor's On Acting.* Crown Publishers, Inc., N.Y., 1970.

Duerr, Edwin. *The Length and Breadth of Acting.* Holt, Rinehart and Winston, N.Y., 1962.

Lewis, Robert. *Slings and Arrows—Theater In My Life.* Stein and Day, N.Y., 1984.

Meckler, Eva. *The New Generation of Acting Teachers.* Penguin Books, N.Y., 1987.

Nagler, A.M. *A Sourcebook In Theatrical History.* Dover Publications, Inc., N.Y.,1952.

Oida, Yoshi. *An Actor Adrift.* Methuen, London, 1994.

Roach, Joseph,R. *The Player's Passion.* University of Michigan Press, 1993.

Wiles, Timothy, J. *The Theater Event—Modern Theories of Performance.* University of Chicago Press, 1980.

Zarrilli, Phillip, ed. *Acting (Re)Considered.* Routledge, N.Y., 1995.

QUINTILIAN

Kennedy, George. *Quintilian.* Twayne Publishers, Inc., 1969.

Watson, Rev. *Quintilian's Institutes of Oratory: Or Education of an Orator.* Trans. John Selby, George Bell and Sons, N.Y., 1892.

AARON HILL

Hill, Aaron. *The Works of the Late Aaron Hill, Esq. in Four Volumes,* London, 1753.

FRANÇOIS DELSARTE

Shawn, Ted. *Every Little Movement.* Dance Horizons, Inc., N.Y., 1954.

Stebbins, Genevieve. *Delsarte System of Dramatic Expression.* Edgar S. Werner, N.Y., 1886.

CONSTANTINE STANISLAVSKI

Benedetti, Jean, *Stanislavski A Biography.* Routledge, N.Y., 1988.

Boleslavsky, Richard, *Acting—The First Six Lessons.* Theater Arts Books, N.Y., 1991.

Edwards, Christine. *The Stanislavsky Heritage.* New York University Press, N.Y., 1965.
Gordon, Mel. *The Stanislavski Technique:Russia.* Applause Theater Book Publishers, N.Y., 1987.
Gorchakov, Nikolai M. *Stanislavski Directs.* Limelight Editions, N.Y., 1991.
Magarshack, David. *Stanislavski, A Life.* Faber and Faber, London, 1986.
Moore, Sonia. *The Stanislavski System.* Penguin Books, N.Y., 1979.
Stanislavski, Constantine. *An Actor Prepares.* Trans. Elizabeth R. Hapgood, Routledge/Theater Arts Books, N.Y., 1936.
Stanislavski, Constantine. *Building A Character.* Trans. Elizabeth, R. Hapgood, Theater Arts Books, N.Y., 1949.
Stanislavski, Constantine. *Creating A Role.* Trans. Elizabeth R. Hapgood, Theater Arts Books, N.Y., 1961.
Stanislavski, Constantine. *My Life In Art.* Trans. J.J. Robbins, Routledge/Theater Arts Books, N.Y., 1994.
Stanislavski, Constantine. *Stanislavski on the Art of the Stage.* Trans. David Magarshack, Faber and Faber Limited, London, 1980.
Troyat, Henri. *Daily Life In Russia Under The Last Tsar.* Stanford University Press, Calif., 1979.

Periodicals

Tulane Drama Review, *Stanislavski and America:1.* Volume 9, Number 1, Fall, 1964.
Tulane Drama Review, *Stanislavski and America:2.* Volume 9, Number 2, Winter 1964.

EVGENI VAKHTANGOV

Gorchakov, Nikolai. *The Vakhtangov School of Stage Art.* Trans. G. Ivanov-Mumjiev, ed. Phyl Griffith, Foreign Languages Publishing House, Moscow.
Simonov, Ruben. *Stanislavski's Protégé: Eugene Vakhtangov.* Trans. and adapted by Miriam Goldina, DBS Publications, Inc., N.Y., 1969.

Periodicals

The Drama Review, *Russian Issue.* Volume 17 Number 2, School of the Arts, New York University, March, 1973.

VSEVOLOD MEYERHOLD

Braun, Edward. *Meyerhold On Theater.* Hill and Wang, N.Y., 1969.

Periodicals

The Drama Review, *Russian Issue.* Volume 17 Number 2, School of the Arts, New York University, March, 1973.

MICHAEL CHEKHOV

Chekhov, Michael. *On The Technique Of Acting.* HarperCollins Publishers, N.Y., 1991.

Chekhov, Michael, *Lessons for the Professional Actor.* Ed. Deidre Hurst Du Prey, Performing Arts Journal Publications, 1992.

THE GROUP THEATER

Clurman, Harold. *All People Are Famous.* Harcourt Brace Jovanovich, N.Y., 1974.

Clurman, Harold. *The Fervent Years.* Harcourt Brace Jovanovich, N.Y., 1975.

Smith, Wendy. *Real Life Drama.* Grove Weidenfeld,N.Y., 1990.

THE METHOD

Easty, Edward Dwight. *On Method Acting.* Ivy Books, N.Y., 1981

Garfield, David. *A Player's PLace.* Macmillan Publishing, N.Y., 1980.

Hagen, Uta. *A Challenge For The Actor.* MacMillan Publishing Co., N.Y., 1991.

Hagen, Uta. *Respect For Acting,* Macmillan Publishing Co., N.Y., 1973.

Hirsch, Foster. *A Method To Their Madness.* W.W. Norton and Compan.y., Inc., New York, 1984.

Lewis, Robert. *Method—Or Madness?.* Samuel French, Inc., N.Y., 1958.

Lewis, Robert. *Advice to the Players.* Theater Communications Group, N.Y., 1980.

Manderino, Ned. *All About Method Acting.* Manderino Books, Calif., 1985

Miller, Alan. *A Passion For Acting,* Backstage Books, New York, 1992.

Vineberg, Steve. *Method Actors.* Schirmer Books, N.Y., 1991.

LEE STRASBERG

Hethmon, Robert. *Strasberg at the Actor's Studio.* Viking Press, N.Y., 1965.

Hull, S. Loraine. *Strasberg's Method.* Ox Bow Publishing, Inc., Conn., 1985.

Strasberg, Lee. *A Dream of Passion.* Little, Brown and Co., Boston, 1987.

Periodicals

Tulane Drama Review, *Stanislavski and America.* Volume 9 Number 1, Fall, 1964.

STELLA ADLER

Adler, Stella. *The Technique of Acting.* Bantam Books, N.Y., 1988.

Periodicals

Tulane Drama Review, *Stanislavski and America.* Volume 9 Number 1, Fall, 1964.

SANFORD MEISNER

Meisner, Sanford and Longwell, Dennis. *Sanford Meisner On Acting.* Random House, Inc., 1987.

Silverberg, Larry. *The Sanford Meisner Approach.* Smith and Kraus Inc., New Hampshire, 1994.

Videotape

Sanford Meisner: The Theater's Best Kept Secret, produced by Kent Paul and directed by Sydney Pollack.

IMPROVISATION

Boal, Augusto. *The Theater of the Oppressed.* Theatre Communications Group, N.Y., 1985.

Boal, Augusto. *The Rainbow of Desire.* Routledge, N.Y., 1995.

Coleman, Janet. *The Compass.* Alfred A. Knopf, N.Y., 1990.

Johnstone, Keith. *Impro.* Routledge Press, N.Y., 1981-1987.

Rudlin, John. *Commedia dell'Arte.* Routledge, N.Y., 1994.

Spolin, Viola. *Improvisation For The Theater.* Northwestern University Press, 1983.

Spolin, Viola. *Theater Games For Rehearsal: A Director's Handbook.* Northwestern University Press, 1985.

Spolin, Viola. *Theater Games For The Classroom: A Teacher's Handbook.* Northwestern University Press, 1986.

Spolin, Viola. *Theater Game File.* Northwestern University Press, 1989.

Sweet, Jeffrey. *Something Wonderful Right Away.* Limelight Editions, 1987.

Yakim, Moni. *Creating A Character.* Applause Books, N.Y., 1993.

BERTOLD BRECHT

Hayman, Ronald. *Brecht: A Biography.* Weidenfeld and Nicolson, London, 1983.

Thomson, Peter and Sacks, Glendyr, ed., *The Cambridge Companion To Brecht,* Cambridge University Press, 1994.

Willett, John, trans. and editor, *Brecht On Theater,* Hill and Wang, N.Y., 1992.

See also under General Acting: *The Theater Event*

Periodicals

Tulane Drama Review, *Stanislavski and America: 2,* Volume 9 number 2, Winter, 1964.

The Drama Review, *Bertold Brecht,* Volume 12 Number 1, Fall 1967.

JERZY GROTOWSKI

Grotowski, Jerzy. *Towards A Poor Theater.* Simon and Schuster, N.Y., 1968.
Kumiega, Jennifer. *The Theatre of Grotowski.* Methuen, London, 1987.
Richards, Thomas. *At Work With Grotowski on Physical Actions.* Routledge, N.Y., 1995
See also under General Acting: *The Theater Event, Acting (Re)Considered*

TADASHI SUZUKI

Suzuki, Tadashi. *The Way of Acting.* Trans. J. Thomas Rimer, Theater Communications Group, N.Y., 1986.
See also under General Acting: *Acting (Re)Considered*

VIDEO BIBLIOGRAPHY

ADLER, STELLA
Shadow of the Thin Man, 1941, directed by W.S. Van Dyke ll.
My Girl Tisa, 1948, directed by Elliott Nugent.

ARTAUD, ANTONIN
Napoléon, 1927, directed by Abel Gance.
The Passion of Joan of Arc, 1928, directed by Carl Dreyer.

CHEKHOV, MICHAEL
Spellbound, 1945, directed by Alfred Hitchcock.

LEWIS, ROBERT
Dragon Seed, 1944, directed by Jack Conway.
Monsieur Verdoux, 1947, directed by Charlie Chaplin.

MEISNER, SANFORD
The Story On Page One, 1959, directed by Clifford Odets.
Sandy Meisner: The Theater's Best Kept Secret, directed by SydneyPollack.

OUSPENSKAYA, MARIA
Dodsworth, 1936, directed by, William Wyler.
Beyond Tomorrow, 1940, directed by A. Edward Sutherland.

STRASBERG, LEE
The Godfather Part II, 1974, directed by Francis Ford Coppola.
The Cassandra Crossing, 1976, directed by George P. Cosmatos.
...And Justice For All, 1979, directed by Norman Jewison.
Going In Style, 1979, directed by Martin Brest.

INDEX

actions, 28, 43-44, 47-51, 55-58, 61, 65, 71, 75, 81, 85, 87-89, 103, 110-111,118, 120, 122-123, 125, 127, 129, 137, 142, 146, 150, 152-153, 162, 167, 176, 183, 187
activities, 123
Actor Prepares, An, 110, 198
Actor's Equity, 172-173
Actor's Studio, xii, 66, 86, 93-94, 99, 106, 114-116, 130, 171, 178
adaptation, 55
adjustment, 61, 80-81, 135
Adler, Jacob, 83, 117
Adler, Luther, 91
Adler, Sara, 117
Adler, Stella, xii, 83, 86-94, 111, 117-125, 127-129, 134, 137-138, 171, 183, 199
Aeschelus, 173
affective memory, 80-81, 85, 88-89, 91, 95, 110-115, 118, 123
air, 2-3
Akalaitis, JoAnn, 178
Akropolis, 161
Alexander Technique, 172-173, 176-177, 179-180, 186
alienation, 149
American Lab Theater, 78-79, 81, 83-84, 108, 117
American Repertory Theater, 173
anger, 2-3, 7, 9, 11
animal, 80, 108-110, 124, 160
Apocalypsis cum figuris, 161
Art of Acting: An Essay, The, 7
Artaud, Antonin, 155-158, 161, 163, 175
Awake And Sing, 90-91, 128
Balinese dancers, 156, 163
beats, 81, 137
Beck, Julian, 161
Beckett, Samuel, 173
Berliner Ensemble, 147-148, 151-152
Berlioz, Hector, 10
Berry, Cicely, 172, 180
Biomechanics, 71-72, 74
black bile, 2-3
Bible, The, 148
Big Knife, The 178
Boal, Augusto, 15, 200
Bogart, Anne, 175
Boleslavsky, Richard, 78-79, 80-81, 88, 95, 117, 197
Brando, Marlon, 93-94, 117, 138, 169
Brecht, Bertold, 75, 91, 147-153, 155-156, 163-164, 169-170, 189, 200-201
Bromberg, J. Edward, 83
Brook, Peter, 162
Brustein, Robert, 173
Büchner, Georg, 148
Building A Character, 110, 198
Burgess, Hovey, 180
Burstyn, Ellen, 176

Calder, Jim, 180
Carnovsky, Morris, 83, 86, 91-92, 118
Chaikin, Joseph, 161
Chairs, The, 154
Chaplin, Charlie, 148
Challenge for the Actor, A , 176
characterization, 60, 65, 70, 81,108-109, 115, 123-124, 164, 172, 182

Chekhov, Anton, 25, 59, 63-64, 84, 92, 164-165, 173, 184
Chekhov, Michael, 63-67, 70, 75, 91, 129, 135, 151, 156, 164, 181, 199
Cherry Orchard, The, 64, 78, 84
Choleric, 2-3
Chrystie Street Settlement House, 79, 84
circle of attention, 32-33
circumstances, 28, 37-44, 46-49, 51-52, 54-55, 57-58, 61, 64-65, 80-81, 85, 89-90, 101, 110-111, 115, 118, 120-124, 126-127, 129-130, 133-137, 146, 150, 167, 176 183, 185, 187
Civic Repertory Theater, 78
Clurman, Harold, 82-84, 86-87, 90, 92, 128, 175, 190
Cobb, Lee J., 109
Coleridge, Samuel Taylor, 149
Commedia del' arte, 69-70, 175
communion, 53, 89, 129, 134, 142, 155, 157, 161, 167, 170
Compass Theater, 139, 179
concentration, 22, 27-28, 31-35, 42, 57, 80, 84, 87, 91, 97, 99-102, 105, 108, 124, 133-134, 164-166, 170-171, 176
Constant Prince, The 161
Constructivism, 69
Copeau, Jacques, 82, 175, 177
Cordle, Dan, 180
Cornell, Katherine, 77
Country Girl, The, 176
Craig, Gordon, 95-96, 116
Crawford, Cheryl, 82, 86-87, 91, 94
Creating A Role, 110-111

Damrosch Institute of Music, 128
Darwin, Charles, 69
Dean, James, 8
decomposing exercises, 12, 27, 30
Delsarte, Francois, 10-13, 15, 17, 22, 27, 30-31, 47-48, 75, 96, 119, 128, 167,188-189, 197
De Niro, Robert, 138
Dialectical Theater, 148
Diderot, Denis, 15
Don Quixote, 65
Dr. Faustus, 161
Dreyer, Carl, 157, 202
Dukakis, Olympia, 180
Durang, Christopher, 178
Duse Elenora, 27
Duvall, Robert, 138

earth, 2-3
Eikenberry, Jill, 187
Einstein, Albert, 69
Eisenstein, Sergei 75
emotion memory, 51-52, 57, 63-64, 80, 86, 88, 90, 95, 113, 118, 176
Epic Theater, 148
Epstein, Alvin, 173
Erik XIV, 63
Esterman, Laura, 176

Farmer, Francis, 86
fear, 7
Feldenkrais, 179, 186
fire, 2-3
Fichandler, Zelda, 180
Fleck, Charlotte, 180
Fo, Dario, 153
Forum Theater, 153
four basic elements, 2
four humours, 2-3, 8
French, Arthur, 176
Freud, Sigmund, 56, 69

Garfield, John (Jules), 86
Garrick, David, xi, 21, 189
Gance, Abel, 157, 202
Gentlewoman, 88
gests, 152
gestus 151, 156
Gogol, Nikolai, 63
Golden Boy, 91
Green, Paul, 82
grief, 7, 9
Grotowski, Jerzy, 75, 154-55, 157-159, 161-164, 169, 189-190, 201
Group Theater, 62, 66, 82-85, 87-92, 94, 111-113, 118, 123, 128-129, 138,153, 190, 199

Hagen, Uta, 176, 199
Hamlet, 37-38, 42-43, 50
hatred, 7, 9
Hawn, Goldie, 8
Hayes, Helen, 77
HB Studios, 176
Hecht, Deborah, 180
Hickey, William, 176
Hill, Aaron, 7-9, 11, 17, 21, 27, 47, 75, 189, 197
Hitchcock, Alfred, 67
House of Connelly, The, 82, 85, 87
Houseman, John, 177
Humour, 2-3
Hunt, Robyn, v, 185

Ibsen, Henrik, 25
Illinois Repertory Theater, 184
imagination, 18, 35-38, 42, 44, 49, 51, 57-58, 62-65, 84, 86, 91, 100-101,108, 110, 118, 120, 126-127, 135, 146, 172, 176, 180
Imperial Dramatic School, 21, 75
industrialism, 69
inner action, 44
inner tempo-rhythm, 57
Inspector General, 63
inspiration, 51
intention, 74, 81, 185
Ionesco, Eugene, 154

Jackson, Ann, 176
jealousy, 7, 9
joy, 7-8
justification, 61-63, 123, 126-127, 183

Kabuki, 69
Kadar, Jan, 78
Kahn, Michael, 177-178
Kass, Peter, 180
Kathakali, 154, 164
Kazan, Elia, 86, 91-94, 138, 178
Keats, John, 9, 28
King Lear, 165
Knight, David, 184
knock on the door, 131

Lan-fang, Mei, 148
lazzi, 70
Le Gallienne, Eva, 78, 176
Lessac, Arthur, 173
Levin, Charles, 173
Lewes, George Henry, 15
Lewis, Robert, 70, 83, 86, 90, 92, 94, 113, 128, 187, 197, 199
Lincoln Center, 66
Linklater, Kristin, 172-174, 176, 180, 185
Living Theater, 161
Lower Depths, The, 78
love, 7, 9
Lunt, Alfred, 77

Mackaye, Steele, 12-15
Maeterlinck, Maurice, 25
magic if, 36-37, 42, 57, 80, 120, 136
Majestic Theater, 90
Marat, 157
Marx Brothers, 157
Marx, Karl, 69, 149
Meisner, Sanford, 83, 86, 90-92, 128-130, 133, 135-138, 142, 171, 176, 200, 202
Melancholic, 2-3
Men In White, 87
Method of Psycho-Physical Actions, 57, 88, 111, 162
Method Or Madness, 66, 199
Meyerhold, Vsevolod, 68-71, 73-75, 147, 149, 154, 163, 175, 189, 198
Miller, Allan, 109
Miller, Arthur, 109
mind, 32
Miss Saigon, 150
Month In The Country, A , 28
Moriarty, Michael, 66-67
Morrison, George, 179
Morrison, Malcolm, 186
Moscow Art Theater (MAT), 23-26, 28, 59-61, 63, 67-68, 77-79, 82, 90, 92, 95, 155
Mother Courage, 151
Mrs. Klein, 176
My Life In Art, 17

Napoleon, 157
Naturalism, 26
Neighborhood Playhouse, 77, 129
Nemirovich-Danchenko, Vladimir, 22-25, 59, 68, 92
New School For Social Research, 93
Newton, Sir Isaac, 69
Nichols, Mike, 179
Nicholson, Jack, 8
nodes, 149
Noh Theater, 69, 163
Norman, Marsha, 178

object of attention, 32-34, 56, 105
objective, 48-52, 55-58, 64, 74, 115, 137, 146, 167, 171, 176, 187
Objective Drama Project 161
obstacles, 137, 167
Ode On A Grecian Urn, 28
Odets, Clifford, 83, 90-92
O'Neill, Eugene, 77-78
Open Theater, 161
Othello 17, 27, 68, 176
Ouspenskaya, Maria 78-81, 88, 95, 108, 112, 202
outer tempo-rhythm, 57
overall action, 123

paraphrasing, 129
particularization, 136-137,
Passion of Joan of Arc, 157, 202
Pavlov, Ivan, 69, 71, 111
Pearson, Steven, 185
Peking Opera, 163
Pendleton, Austin, 176
phlegm, 2-3
Phlegmatic, 3
Picasso, Pablo, 68
pity, 7-9
plastiques, 158
Plato, 50
Popova, L., 69
preceding incident, 124
preparation, 136-137
private moment, 105-107, 115
Provincetown Players, 83
Provincetown Playhouse, 77

Pryce, Jonathan, 150
psychological gesture, 66-67, 151, 156
Psychology of the Emotions, 52, 80
public solitude, 34, 42, 57, 105, 134

Quintilian, 4-9, 12, 15, 17, 21, 75, 113, 156, 169, 189

Rappaport, 129
Raether, Richard, 181
reality of doing, 131
realization, 74
red blood, 2-3
Refusal of the Action, (Meyerhold), 74
relaxation, 12, 27-31, 33, 42, 57, 80, 96-97, 99-101, 108, 119-120, 140, 167, 171
Respect for Acting, 176, 199
Resurrection, 176
Rhetoric, 4
Ribot, Théodule, 52, 80
Riccoboni, Luigi, 15
Richard The Third, 66
RMS Majestic, 77
Rosato, Mary Lou, 180

Salvini, Tomasso, 27
Sanguine, 3
scorn, 7, 9
Seagull, The, 25, 68,
Second City, 139
sense memory, 34-35, 52, 57, 64, 80, 84, 90, 100-105, 108, 111-112, 114, 120, 143, 171, 176, 178
sense of truth, 7, 37, 46, 57, 125, 177
Serban, Andrei, 175
Shakespeare, William, 17, 25, 42, 66, 86, 138, 164-165, 167, 173, 176-177, 183-184, 187
Shapiro, Mel, 66
Shchepkin, Mikhail, 19-20, 22
Shooting the Bow, 72-73
Shop On Main Street, The, 78
Siakuntala, 154
Sills, Paul, 139, 179
Skinner, Edith, 180
Slavic Bazaar, 22
Solon, ix-x
Spellbound, 67
Spolin, Viola, 121, 139-140, 146, 176, 179, 200
Stanislavski, Constantine, xiii, 12, 16-28, 30-32, 34, 36, 38, 40, 44, 48, 50-63, 67-69, 74-75, 78-82, 84, 87-92, 94-96, 99-100, 105, 108, 110-111, 113-114, 118-120, 122-123, 127-129, 134, 136-139, 142, 146-148, 150, 152, 155, 157, 161-165, 167, 169-171, 173-176, 179, 181, 184-185, 187, 189-190, 197-198
Strasberg, Lee, xi, 62, 79-100, 105, 108, 111, 113, 115-116, 118-119, 123, 128, 130, 134, 138, 171, 176, 178-179, 199
Stoddard, Eunice, 83
Story Theater, 179
strategies, 137
Stravinski, Igor, 68
Streep, Meryl, 187
Strindberg, August, 63
Stritch, Elaine, 183
subconscious, 51
subtext, 54, 183
Sudakov, 129
super-objective, 50-51, 81, 95, 110
Sussel, Deborah, 172
Suzuki, Tadashi, xiii, 70, 163-165, 167-168, 170, 172, 175, 178, 180, 185, 189-190, 201

T'ai chi, 173
Taylor, Frederick, 70
tempo rhythm, 55-57, 80, 109, 124
Theater of Cruelty, 156, 157
Theater Games, 121, 139, 141, 146, 176, 180
Theater Guild, 78, 83, 128
The Poor Theater 155
Theater of Sources, 162
Theater of Thirteen Rows, 154
Thespis, ix, 29-37, 38-40, 42-49, 51-57
Tone, Franchot, 83
Three Sisters, The, 68
Through-line-of-action, 51, 123
Trigorin, 25,
Trojan Women, The, 166-167
Tsar Fyodor, 24, 78
Turgenev, Ivan, 28
Twelfth Night, 62

Über-marionette, 95-96

V-effect, 149-150
Vakhtangov, Evgeni, 60-63, 67, 74-75, 79-81, 84, 87, 90, 94-95, 123, 129, 135, 138, 175, 189, 198
Verfremdung, 149, 153
Vertov, Dziga, 69, 148
visualization, 65

Waiting For Godot, 173
Waiting For Lefty, 90-91, 153
Walker, Jewell, 165
Washington Square Players, 77-78
water, 2-3
Weaver, Sigourney, 187
Wedekind, Frank, 148
Weigel, Helene, 151
Weill, Kurt, 91
Welles, Orson, 173
Who's Afraid of Virginia Woolf?, 176
Wideman, Beverly, 180
Wilson, Elizabeth, 176
Winkler, Henry, 187
wonder, 7, 9
word repetition game, 131
Workcenter of Jerzy Grotowski, 162
Wright, Amy, 176
Wright, Nicholas, 176

Yale Repertoy Theater, 187
Yale School of Drama, 172-173, 187
yellow bile, 2-3
Yount, Shane Ann, 180

Zeus, 16